On Your Mark,
Get Set,
Teach!

All the best !! :-)

Lisa F. Willi
2008

On Your Mark, Get Set, Teach!

The *Must Have* Guide For *New* Teachers

Lisa Funari Willever
Lisa Battinelli

Foreword by
Donald Greenwood

Franklin Mason Press

Cover Design by Peri Poloni, Knockout Design, Cameron Park, CA
www.knockoutbooks.com

Franklin Mason Press ISBN 0-9679227-5-5
Library of Congress Control Number: 2002109697

Editorial staff Marcia Jacobs, Linda Funari, and Catherine Funari

www.franklinmasonpress.com

Table of Contents

Foreword   9

By Mr. Donald Greenwood, Retired Supervisor,
Principal, and Teacher.

Chapter One   11
Welcome To The Big Desk

Introduction and summary of each chapter.

Chapter Two   23
It's What You Know *and Who You Know*

The importance of establishing relationships with
everyone in your school community, from secretaries
to custodians.

Chapter Three   35
Know What You Teach and Teach What You Know

It is important to quickly acquaint yourself with the
curriculum you will be required to teach.

Chapter Four   41
A Place For Everything and Everything In Its Place

Organization is an important key to establishing a
successful teaching career. Invest the time into
setting up a well-organized room and detailed
system of keeping records.

Chapter Five   49
Walk A Mile In Their Shoes *or Spend A Moment In Their Desks*

This chapter concentrates on the physical characteristics of
the classroom, knowing what your students will be able to
see and hear from their seats.

Chapter Six   57
Please Report To The Principal's Office

> Strategies to make a strong first impression, work-
> ing with an administrator, and establishing a good
> rapport.

Chapter Seven   65
A Diamond In The Rough

> Parents can be your strongest ally and it is up to
> you to cultivate a positive, working relationship.
> Suggestions for keeping the lines of communication
> open and making the most of the teacher-parent
> partnership.

Chapter Eight   71
A Penny For Their Thoughts

> Getting to know your students is priceless and
> essential to being a successful teacher. Use the
> strategies in this chapter to connect with each
> student in your class.

Chapter Nine   79
Do As I Say...Period

> Regardless of your proficiency in a given subject
> area, without successful classroom management,
> instruction will be ineffective. Tips on establishing
> appropriate classroom rules and consequences.

Chapter Ten   95
How Do I Assess Thee? Let Me Count The Ways

> Assessment is one of the most controversial areas
> of education. The most effective approach is to
> combine as many methods as possible. This
> chapter discusses those various methods.

Chapter Eleven   103
Come One, Come All

Special events make school a memorable place for
students. Whether it is Back to School Night, Field
Day or a School Play, do your best to support the
event.

Chapter Twelve   119
On The Road Again

From choosing a destination to scheduling, this
chapter provides everything necessary for a
wonderful outing.

Chapter Thirteen   129
The Nuts And Bolts

This chapter is divided into two sections, Look
Before You Leap and He Said, She Said. This
chapter covers the liabilities facing educators,
workplace conduct, and interpersonal relationships.

Chapter Fourteen   139
To Stay Or Not To Stay...This Is The Question

Finding a job is wonderful, finding the right job can
be magical. At the end of your first year you
should conduct your own evaluation and determine
if you should stay where you are or look elsewhere.

Chapter Fifteen   153
May We Suggest

A comprehensive chapter devoted to providing
useful resources that will be of value to a new
teacher. You will find websites, free offers for
teachers, and a directory of wonderful educational
supply stores.

To my beautiful children, Jessica and Patrick and my
always supportive husband, Todd.
Also, to my teaching mentor, Vicki...LW

To my wonderful family and my colleagues in the
River Edge School System who continue to inspire and
support me in an ongoing learning process...LB

About The Authors

Lisa Funari Willever is a lifelong resident of Trenton, New Jersey and a former fourth grade teacher in the Trenton Public School District. As a graduate of The College of New Jersey (formerly Trenton State College) she is a member of the New Jersey Reading Association and the Society of Children's Book Writers and Illustrators. Currently, a full-time writer, she is the author of several children's books, including *Where Do Snowmen Go, You Can't Walk A Fish, Everybody Moos at Cows, Chumpkin, The Easter Chicken, Maximilian The Great, Miracle On Theodore's Street,* and *The Culprit Was a Fly.* Her husband, Todd, is a Firefighter in the city of Trenton and the co-author of *Miracle On Theodore's Street.* They are the proud parents of three year old Jessica and two year old Patrick.

Lisa Battinelli is a graduate of The College of New Jersey (formerly Trenton State College) and Long Island University where she received her Master's Degree in Reading. She is a lifelong resident of Bergen County, New Jersey and a member of the New Jersey Education Association. Lisa teaches in River Edge, New Jersey and was named Teacher of the Year in 1995-96. Her husband, Peter, is a commodities broker in Greenwich, Connecticut and they are the proud parents of Grace Lesley.

Foreword

As a first year teacher, you are about to enter the most rewarding profession in the world. You will be fostering the intellectual growth of students who look to you for knowledge, compassion, understanding and acceptance. Be proud, you are a teacher. Enter the profession with self-confidence and enthusiasm. Do not think of teaching as a job. Consider this a truly magnificent opportunity to make a difference in the lives of your students. You are not only building the future of our country, but the futures of the individual students in your classroom.

As a building principal, I have had the opportunity to work with many first year teachers. I have no doubt that you are filled with anxiety and have many questions and concerns. Believe me, this is natural and the anxiety will quickly disappear as you begin each day. Remember, you have been here before as a first grader, a freshman in high school, and a freshman in college. I am sure you had many concerns as you approached these new phases of your life, yet you overcame, survived, and learned through experience. Let experience be your guide and self-confidence will flourish.

The authors, two very experienced and successful classroom teachers, offer you a multitude of situations, challenges, and solutions for effective teaching. Most important, they offer you advice based on the realism of classroom experience.

Of significant importance is Chapter 8, *A Penny For Their Thoughts.* A successful teacher utilizes all of the knowledge gained after four years of digesting theory, comprehending research, and participating in field experiences. You will be successful, however, if you remember the three most important words, **know your students.** A teacher must know each student's individual ability levels, how they learn best, their sensitivity level, how they react to the tone of your voice, and their family backgrounds. If you know your students, you will know what to teach and how to teach it to them.

Foreword

The incorporation of effective classroom management techniques is essential to establish and maintain an effective learning environment. The authors provide you with many excellent suggestions in Chapter 9, *Do As I Say...Period.* Be creative and use your imagination to ensure that the end result is fun and productive.

In Chapter 10, *How Do I Assess Thee? Let Me Count The Ways,* you will be introduced to the various forms of assessment. This is vitally important in order to evaluate what your students have learned and how effective your lessons were. Remember, every lesson will not be successful. When this occurs, use your creativity to alter your technique.

When it comes to dealing with parents, refer to Chapter 7, *A Diamond In The Rough*, for excellent approaches. Parents need to know that you are supportive, and eager to help their child.

I remember, my first day of teaching. I was a fourth grade teacher assigned to Room 14 with 44 students. Talk about anxiety! As the students entered the room, however, the anxiety disappeared and the excitement of having my very own class was overwhelming. At the end of the day, as I sat in my empty classroom, several teachers stopped by to see how my first day went. "Fantastic," I replied. My career as a teacher was off to a magnificent start and I realized all of the what-if's were unnecessary.

Once the school year begins, do not dwell on all of the things that can go wrong. Concentrate on all of the exciting things you will accomplish with your students. Maintain a high level of self-confidence and use this book to ease your anxiety.

As a student teaching supervisor, I can assure you that you are more prepared than you realize. This is not to say that all of your days will be successful; they won't. The important thing to remember is you have the knowledge to fix what went wrong. You also have many people and resources to help you in your time of need. Use them and enjoy your new career!

Donald Greenwood
Retired Supervisor, Principal, and Teacher

Chapter 1

<u>Welcome to the Big Desk</u>

If you have just landed your first position as a teacher, congratulations! The information included in this book will guide you through your first year, addressing many issues pertinent to new teachers. If you are currently studying to be a teacher or looking for your first position, this book will provide you with a new perspective on education. For the first time, you will be the Teacher, not a student. We would like to be the first to welcome you to the Big Desk!

The purpose of this book is simple and its strength is not in new, groundbreaking techniques. On the contrary, this book contains methods, tips, and techniques used by successful teachers on a daily basis. Clearly, we have not reinvented the wheel. We have simply considered the many questions new teachers often contemplate and have attempted to provide clear, step-by-step answers.

The format is informal and designed to be conversational in nature. *On Your Mark, Get Set, Teach* is a dialogue between two experienced teachers and you, the reader. Imagine having the opportunity to sit down with two veteran teachers and ask as many questions as you would like, without being judged or feeling that a question was silly. More importantly, you will find the answers to questions you have yet to discover.

This book can be used as a primer for your first teaching experience or as a reference guide when specific information is needed. While your college education provides necessary theories required to teach, even the most prestigious program cannot provide you with experience. As you begin your new career, you will draw upon your college courses and student teaching experiences; however, you will find that real classroom experience will become your most valuable point of reference.

The Learning Curve

For any new career, there is a learning curve and teachers are not exempt. Do not be afraid to make a mistake if you are willing to learn from it. Appreciate all feedback, whether complimentary or critical. Have an open mind and learn to adjust to the many variables involved in day-to-day teaching. Once you have read the information in this book, let common sense be your guide and conduct yourself as a professional under *all* circumstances.

As you begin reading, you will quickly notice that this book is the result of two completely different teaching experiences, one urban and one suburban. It is important to understand that each school district is different and within a district, each school is different. For that reason, ***nothing in this book can be applied to every scenario in every school. We must emphasize that the application of any content is only recommended if it complies with your school's policies.*** It is your responsibility to acquaint yourself with your new environment, learning policies, procedures, and protocol. Use these ideas as a tool, in conjunction with common sense, for *your* particular school environment.

There is little consensus in the world of education. Some schools encourage parents to visit frequently, join the class, and become an active part of their child's education. Other schools may frown upon having parents in the classroom and do not permit this type of interaction. Some schools rely on standardized testing and basal readers. Others utilize portfolio assessment and whole language instruction. Before implementing any of the suggestions you find in this book and in case you were daydreaming through the first warnings, be sure that they comply with your school's policies and that you are comfortable with them.

It Seems Like Yesterday...

As we sat down to write this book, we remembered the summer before our first teaching positions were to begin. We were about to embark on a journey that involved years of preparation and hard work. Within days of each other, we were both hired as second grade teachers. Lisa B. would be working in River Edge, New Jersey, a small, suburban district. Lisa F. would be working in Trenton, New Jersey, a large, inner-city district. Other than grade level, our experiences would be anything but similar.

Upon receiving the good news, we were ecstatic. It was almost too good to be true. We had never experienced this level of accomplishment and told everyone we knew and even some people we didn't. For a week we were on top of the world and then, reality hit. Somehow, we never saw it coming.

By the end of July, we were in, for lack of medical terminology, an anxiety-triggered daze. We called each other in a panic and dreamed up crazy questions. Were we ready? Did we choose the right major? Would we be effective? What if the students asked a question and we didn't know the answer? The list went on. In our hearts we knew we had chosen the right major, we believed we were ready, and we hoped we would be effective. Most importantly, we remembered that the teacher's edition of the textbooks *had the answers!*

We stopped by our new schools to gather the curriculum guides and teacher's manuals. For hours, we would pour through the curriculum and read each lesson in the books. Trips to the mall were quickly replaced by trips to the teacher supply stores. It was as if we were playing beat the clock and the countdown to the first day of school had begun. Tension was mounting and we felt like runners on a starting block, except it seemed like they would yell, "On your mark, get set, TEACH!"

Within weeks, we felt as if we had a handle on the curriculum and the units we would be teaching. As soon as we felt confident with the material, however, we found something else to worry about. Actually, we outdid ourselves and found numerous things to worry about. Would the other teachers like us? Would the students like us? Would the parents like us? You probably notice the pattern developing. Looking back, these fears were no different than those of anyone about to start a new career. You are concerned about the impression you will make and hope you manage to utter something slightly intelligent. While the environment of a school will feel familiar, unless you teach in a school you once attended, *you will be the new kid on the block.*

By August, we had our room assignments and went to our respective schools almost every day. We spent days cleaning and discarding materials that accumulated over the years, then organizing and decorating our rooms. We met many staff members and even a few parents. That summer, we learned two important lessons. First, we learned the value of the school secretary, especially to a new teacher. This, clearly, is the person who keeps the whole operation running smoothly. There are many things a school could get by without and a secretary is not one of them. We also learned that we would need to work to earn the respect of our colleagues and that not everyone would bring out the welcome mat.

In the weeks before school starts, teachers decorate their rooms and organize materials. They spend days and weeks preparing for the new school year on their own time. For this reason, they come and go as their schedules permit. Some will plan on spending a whole day, while others may only have an hour or two. You will surely feel overwhelmed as you see so many strangers coming and going. Many will approach you and introduce themselves. Some will appear to be distant. You may even feel like some are trying to initiate you into a sorority before anyone else initiates you. We quickly learned to be pleasant and professional, reserving judgment until we had an opportunity to get to know each person.

During the weeks before school starts and the weeks right after, many people, especially parents, will want to get to know you. The reality of the situation is that many parents will be apprehensive about leaving their child with a new teacher. This is a natural reaction and not something you want to take personally. When parents approach you, listen to their concerns and let them know that you are interested.

As any college graduate knows, securing a position in your field is a milestone and a relief. Unfortunately, it can also be a significant source of anxiety. For a new teacher, there is a sense of familiarity, as your new career is *in a school*. By the time you reach this point, you will have spent nearly 20 years in a variety of schools. The difference is however, that during those years, you were a student. Your environment may seem familiar, but as a teacher your role is dramatically different. Use this book to understand what is expected of you, to navigate through uncharted territory, and to ease some of the anxieties you will, no doubt, experience.

The first day of school for a new teacher, can be trying, even under the best of circumstances. My first day as a teacher was memorable, to say the least.

As the students entered my second grade classroom, a swarm of parents and grandparents followed behind them. I tried to remain calm on the outside, even though my instincts told me to run to the nearest exit.

I had spent days making name tags for their desks and was ready to escort each child to his or her seat. I knew I was in trouble when the first 3 names did not ring a bell. It became painfully apparent that I had been given the wrong class list.

One little boy started to cry when he saw that the name on his desk was not his. Another little girl refused to come in the room because she wanted to go back to first grade. As soon as I calmed the children down, a little boy began to vomit. I felt the eyes of each parent watching my every move. In an attempt to appear as though I had everything under control, I grabbed a book of riddles. By the second riddle, the children and their families were laughing and everyone seemed at ease. I quickly learned that what can go wrong, will, and that humor can ease the most trying situations. -LW

Each chapter is designed to address the needs of a first year teacher and includes personal stories, suggestions, and advice. As mentioned earlier, this book will prepare you for the transition to school as a workplace. The following is a summary of each chapter, highlighting the different topics discussed. Keep in mind that all schools are different and what works in one, may not work in another. Experience will be your best mentor, but this information will guide you as you gain that experience.

Chapter 2
It's What You Know *and Who You Know*

This chapter deals with the importance of establishing relationships with everyone in your school community, from the secretary to the custodians and respecting the role each person plays in the success of a school. The support staff is, without a doubt, the most overlooked population in the building. Make it a point to introduce yourself to the people who keep the building clean and warm, the people who provide meals for your students, and the people who transport your students safely. Without their contributions, you would not be able to perform your job.

Chapter 3
Know What You Teach and Teach What You Know

In a perfect world, a teacher would be an expert in every subject he or she is required to teach. In reality, many teachers, especially at the elementary level, teach a variety of subjects. It is important to quickly acquaint yourself with the curriculum you will be responsible for teaching and to learn as much about it as possible. The teacher's edition of each textbook will break units into lessons, offer tips and strategies, extension activities, and a timeline. While it is often impossible to follow a timeline, it serves as a guide to gauge progress.

You should determine where your interests lie and see what you can add to the lessons, by way of personal experiences, travel, or knowledge of material. Use your own base of knowledge to enhance your units.

Chapter 4
A Place For Everything and Everything In Its Place

Organization is a key element of a successful teaching career. Invest the time into setting up a well-organized room with detailed records and your investment will pay off. The first year is a bit overwhelming and you will want to record grades, performance, behavior, communication with parents and administrators, and important dates. This chapter goes beyond keeping a tidy classroom; it also includes documenting everything and keeping critical papers in a secure, safe place.

Chapter 5
Walk A Mile In Their Shoes
or Spend A Moment In Their Desks

It is imperative that you know what the students will be able to see and hear from their seats, whether they will be able to move about without disturbing others, and possible distractions that may exist. This chapter concentrates on the physical characteristics of the classroom and encourages new teachers to sit in each desk for a moment, once the room is set up. Viewing the room from your students' perspective is also helpful when you begin decorating. You will want to place educational decorations where your students' eyes will wander. This is a clever way to capitalize on *occasional daydreaming.*

Chapter 6
Please Report To The Principal's Office

The relationship you establish with your administrators is very important. These are delicate, professional relationships and require a great deal of effort. This chapter will provide strategies to handle the challenge, establish a good rapport, and make a strong first impression. It also deals with issues of observations, disciplinary action, and rare, but possible lawsuits.

Chapter 7
A Diamond In The Rough

As the first day of school approaches, you should view each relationship with a parent as a diamond in the rough. It is up to you to welcome your students and their parents and cultivate positive, working relationships. Parents can be your strongest ally, and you should let them know that you consider them as partners in the education of their child. Keep the lines of communication open when issues arise *and when things are going well.*

Chapter 8
A Penny For Their Thoughts

The ability to get to know your students is priceless and essential to being a successful teacher. Each student is a member of the class, but they are also individuals. They each arrive with their own personality, temperament, likes, dislikes, and abilities. By getting to know them and letting them know you, you will be able to respond to their needs effectively. This chapter focuses on the worthwhile task of getting to know each student as an individual.

Chapter 9
Do As I Say...Period

While this may sound like something your parents once said, you must remember that while your students are in school, you are the authority figure. You will be responsible for establishing classroom policies and enforcing consistent consequences in conjunction with your school's rules. Regardless of your proficiency in a given subject area, without successful classroom management, instruction will be ineffective. Your students are to do as they are told, no questions asked. You must be firm and understand that you will not always be their favorite person. While it may sound cliche, *it is for their own good.*

Chapter 10
How Do I Assess Thee? Let Me Count The Ways

Assessment is probably the most controversial area of education. Each year new standards are introduced and it is difficult to keep up. The most effective form of assessment uses a variety of methods. It is impossible to accurately measure student understanding using only one form of assessment. All students will not excel in the same format, so various methods need to be utilized. This chapter explains the various forms of assessment and reminds teachers that assessment is measuring student growth and understanding, not mastery of the evaluation itself.

Chapter 11
Come One, Come All

Special Events make school a memorable place. They are extremely important to students and their parents and should be treated as such. Whether it is Back To School Night, a bake sale, a school play, or field day, you should do your best to support the event. This is an area where all students, even those with little academic confidence, can enjoy and one that often brings out the best in the most challenging students. Invite parents whenever possible and, if the situation warrants, share your events with the local media. Your students may not remember the day you introduced them to an octagon, but they will remember the day you ran in a three-legged race. Do your best to make these days as special and meaningful as possible.

Chapter 12
On The Road Again

Field trips, whether walking or traveling by bus, can be a tremendous opportunity to apply material your students have learned in the classroom. Unfortunately, they are also a tremendous responsibility and not to be taken lightly. Preparation, from the selection of a destination, number of parents attending, and the detailed schedule, will ensure a safe trip. In addition to the details, your students must know what you expect of them in terms of behavior. You should also be sure that each student has returned a permission slip before he or she is permitted to leave the building. While it can be heartbreaking to leave a crying second grader behind on trip day, the consequences of bringing a student without written permission, could end your career.

Chapter 13
<u>The Nuts And Bolts</u>

This chapter is broken into two sections, **Look Before You Leap** and **He Said, She Said.** In **Look Before You Leap**, we discuss strategies to acclimate yourself to your new workplace. As a teacher, a school is your place of employment, and you must conduct yourself as a professional and follow all policies. When working with children, you must constantly be aware of your conduct and the liabilities that exist.

In **He Said, She Said**, we discuss the dynamics of the relationships that exist within the building. New teachers must delicately navigate their way through gossip, rumor, and politics without becoming involved. While this is good advice for all teachers, it is essential for a new teacher.

Chapter 14
<u>To Stay or Not To Stay...*That Is The Question*</u>

When you have completed your first year, you will have been observed and scrutinized by dozens of people. You will be evaluated on your performance, classroom management, and let's face it, even your shoes! Before the year is over, you may be offered a contract for the following year. It is now time to conduct your own evaluation and determine if you want to stay. You need to be honest and determine if the school is right for you; if you should stay or look for another school. One of the worst decisions you can make is to stay in a building where you are unhappy or stressed. Finding a job is wonderful, but finding the right job can be magical. If your school does not fit your needs, continue searching and avoid a premature case of teacher burnout.

Chapter 15
<u>May We Suggest?</u>

Resources, resources, and more resources. Do you need to find a great teacher supply store in your area? Do you need to find free materials for your classroom? Do you need to plan an educational trip? Would you like to speak to other new teachers? If the answer is yes, this is the chapter for you. You will find a variety of resources that will help you prepare for one of the most important jobs on the planet, *educating our future.*

As you begin your journey into the world of education, you will have great days and not-so-great days. It is important to remember that every teacher experiences this phenomenon. As in life, some days just seem to be harder than others. Follow the tips in this book and learn to anticipate problems, diagnose causes, and apply solutions.

At the same time, we must provide you with the inevitable fine print. All advice provided will not apply to every new teacher in every situation. Before applying any advice from this book, be sure that it complies with school codes and policies. All advice is given with the best of intentions and for information only.

Having said that, we wish you a wonderful first year.

Lisa & Lisa

On Your Mark, Get Set, Teach!

Chapter 2

It's What You Know *and* *Who You Know*

Before you are hired as a classroom teacher, you probably never think about the support staff with whom you will be working. When most people think of a school, they think of a principal and the teachers. As a first year teacher, it is imperative that you recognize the contributions of *everyone* in your building and your district.

Secretaries

We'll start with one of the most important individuals in a school, the Secretary. On occasion, new teachers make the mistake of believing they know more than staff members who may not have a college degree. This is a serious mistake. Never underestimate how helpful a secretary can be, especially when you are not familiar with the routine you will be expected to follow.

A secretary is the lifeline of the school and can be a tremendous ally if you take the time to form a positive working relationship. Secretaries not only know their own job responsibilities, they also know the responsibilities of everyone else. This is the person to whom you will bring many of your questions and more importantly, this is where you will find most of your answers. Until you complete your first full year, it will be hard to imagine the amount of paperwork you will face. Upon first glance, you will no doubt have many questions and at times you will miss deadlines. A secretary can gently remind and help you or report you to the principal. When a situation arises with a parent, a secretary is often the first person the parent meets. More often than not, a secretary can diffuse a tense situation or warn you as to what is developing. The following tips will help you to establish and cultivate this valuable relationship with your school secretaries:

❖ Be pleasant and helpful whenever possible. If you are on your way out for lunch, ask the secretaries if they would like you to bring anything back. Many secretaries never have a chance to leave the building and frequently eat lunch at their desks.

❖ If you are on a break and the secretary is alone, ask if he or she needs you to watch the office for a moment. Your secretary may want to use the restroom, stretch his or her legs, or make a private phone call.

❖ Do not ask questions when a secretary is in the middle of ten activities. If you have complicated questions, arrive early, before the school day begins or wait until the end of the day. The office is, by far, the most hectic zone of the building and you need to appreciate the stress secretaries are under.

❖ Turn in all required paperwork early. If the secretary finds mistakes or omissions, you will have time to make corrections. Promptness and accuracy are the sign of a professional.

❖ When sending students to the office, be sure they understand exactly what they have been sent for or send a clear note. All too often a secretary must play 20 questions with a first grader who has forgotten the message on the way to the office.

❖ When your school secretary does help you, drop a little note on his or her desk to show your appreciation. *A bagel or muffin in the morning isn't a bad idea either!*

❖ Remind your students to show the secretaries the same respect that they show you. If a secretary assists them, have them write a thank you note.

Custodians

When you think of the staff members that keep a school running, the custodians should immediately come to mind. A school custodian is one of the most unappreciated people in the building. Most people go about their day, giving very little thought to the work performed by a custodian, *until they need one.* Custodians keep the building cool or warm, change light bulbs so your students can see, spread salt when it snows, and mow the grass. They also help you move things, hang things, and fix things that break at the most inopportune times. Custodians are responsible for boilers, heating and cooling, plumbing, and electricity. They keep the building safe and in running order. To establish a positive relationship, try the following:

❖   If a piece of equipment, such as an overhead projector or pencil sharpener breaks, always *ask* if the custodian would mind taking a look at it. If he or she does assist you, send a thank you note.

❖   If the building is too hot or too cold, do not start sending a trail of children to the custodian's office. If you are uncomfortable, chances are that other teachers are, too. Let the veteran teachers bring it to their attention.

❖   If you need a custodian immediately, send a note explaining the situation and wait patiently. If you do not receive immediate assistance, ask the secretary for assistance. Do not report a custodian to the principal. He or she may be involved in another situation or may not have been in the office when the message was sent. A secretary will be able to assess the urgency and contact the custodian.

❖   If there is a safety concern in your room, such as an exposed wire, a dangling light, or a strange odor, remove the children and report it to the secretary. **It is always better to err on the side of caution.**

Cleaning Staff

In addition to the custodians, you must remember the cleaning staff. Most schools have people who come in to clean the building, before and after school. They are paid much less than classroom teachers, but their work is extremely important. When you arrive to a clean, orderly school in the morning, it is because someone worked very hard to keep it that way. When the glitter pumpkins your students labored over leave mounds of orange glitter all over your room, you will begin to understand the importance of the cleaning staff.

The following are some tips for working with the cleaning staff:

❖   Try to leave your room as neat as possible. The students should play an active role in keeping the classroom orderly. Do not train them to believe that someone else will clean up after them.

❖   Do not fill garbage bags to the point where they are too heavy to be lifted.

❖   Ask if there is anything you can do to make their job easier, such as placing garbage by the door or emptying the pencil sharpener.

Cafeteria Staff

If you are not required to oversee student lunch or recess, your school may have a cafeteria staff. Depending upon the school, this staff may prepare the lunches, oversee the lunch tables, and even direct recess. It is a good idea to get to know the cafeteria staff. They are with your students during their 'free time' and can provide you with important insight regarding their behavior when you are not present. They can warn you about potential conflicts among students or let you know if a student is being harassed by others. They often go the extra mile to ensure that each student has a nutritious lunch and some quality down time, during the noisiest portion of the day. Remember the following when dealing with the lunch staff:

❖ Learn their names and make sure your students address them properly.

❖ Ask for daily behavior reports and insist that your students behave in the lunchroom. They must show the lunch staff the same respect they show you.

❖ Do not *dump* your class in the lunchroom and believe that whatever occurs during lunch is not your responsibility. If a student's behavior is inappropriate, record it and mention it to the parent.

School Nurse

Another vital staff member is the School Nurse. Whether your school has a full time or a part time nurse, he or she deserves the same respect as other staff members. A school nurse does much more than take temperatures and clean scrapes. He or she is a vital part of the Child Study Team. A nurse must see every student for their height, weight, hearing and vision tests, keep track of students that miss evaluations as well as new students entering the building. They see children who must have medicine dispensed and recorded at the same time everyday and those who have serious illnesses or disabilities.

At the same time, the nurse sees numerous children with complaints that range from a sore throat to severe asthma attacks. He or she needs to be able to assess the severity of an illness and determine when to call a parent. The nurse's office is a very busy place and the nurse has a great deal of responsibility *and liability.*

If your school does not have a full-time nurse on duty during school hours, be sure to find out the procedures for dealing with sick or injured students. You do not want to wait until you are in the middle of a crisis to start asking where help is available.

During my first year, as a second grade teacher, a very serious situation arose. It was the end of the day and the children were working on a lesson in their handwriting books. A little girl in the back of the room laid her head down on her desk. In an inner-city school, this was not uncommon. Some of the students live with older grandparents and great-grandparents, some were in foster homes, and many were victims of neglect. I was warned by other teachers that this may occur and to be sensitive to their situations. I knew that this particular little girl was under a great deal of stress. She had gradually grown quite depressed and her grandmother informed me that she had not been sleeping.

For weeks, she had been taking little naps in class. Aware of the situation, I didn't wake her up. The students put their handwriting books away and cleared their desks to listen to the book I had been reading to them. The little girl continued to sleep. When it was time to pack up to go home, I went over and gently tapped her arm. She didn't respond. I stroked her cheek and called her name repeatedly, still she did not respond. Suddenly, my heart dropped and I remember another little girl, calling out in a thick Liberian accent, "Maybe she's dead!"

I immediately sent for the nurse and called for the teacher next door. The teacher nudged her and even stood her up, yet she was still unresponsive. I returned her to her desk and placed my finger under her nose, praying that she was breathing. Within moments, the nurse arrived and a call was placed to 9-1-1. The paramedics assessed her and she was immediately hooked up to oxygen.

> *The principal covered my class and I followed the ambulance to the hospital. As I drove to the hospital, panic created dreadful images in my mind. I envisioned the headline in the newspapers, "New Teacher Kills Student." I couldn't imagine what had happened. I ran into the emergency room and watched them work on her. I do not have a degree in medicine, but it was explained to me that she was so upset, she fell into a self-induced coma. She fully recovered and I survived, what I still consider to be, the scariest moment of my career. - LW*

The following are some tips for a pleasant working relationship with the school nurse:

❖ Always be mindful of the nurse's lunch and prep periods. Keep these times in a visible place near your desk. If a student complains of a sore throat or a runny nose, try to wait until the nurse is back in the office before sending the student. Some students may make-up illnesses to get out of classwork or for attention; however, ***if you have any doubt about the severity of an illness, send the child immediately***.

❖ If a serious situation arises, remain calm, for the sake of the affected student and also for your class. Do not panic, take a deep breath and immediately send for the school nurse. Ask a teacher nearby for assistance, but continue to remain calm. Do not move an injured student, as you could cause further injury.

❖ It is a good idea to know basic first aid, but always consult the school nurse.

❖ When you send a student to the nurse, provide vital information, including the child's name, class, and complaint. The nurse may not know every student and does not have time to play detective.

❖ If a student needs to have medicine dispensed from the nurse at a specific time, be sure to send the student on time. It is not the nurse's responsibility to search for students.

❖ Try to make all activities as safe as possible. Reducing the likelihood of injury and taking steps to prevent accidents will eliminate possible problems.

❖ If you need something from the nurse, be patient. Do not expect everything to be dropped the moment you ask a question.

> *As a teacher, the previously mentioned situation presented a number of issues, first and foremost, the well-being of the student. I followed all of the correct procedures and ensured that the nurse was alerted as soon as the severity of the situation was discovered.*
>
> *Second, I was able to keep 23 second graders calm throughout the ordeal. I remember, as I subtly checked for a pulse, telling my class that she sure was a sound sleeper. While I was in a complete panic on the inside, it was imperative that I appear calm for the sake of the other students.*
>
> *Third, when I returned to the school, I was told that the class was very scared and upset. That evening, I called every student and reassured them that their friend was okay and would be returning soon. She never fell into a coma again, however, we all held our breath whenever she took a*

Specialists or Special Area Teachers

Throughout the day, your students will receive instruction from a number of specialists or special area teachers, including Physical Education, Library, Art, Music, Instrumentals, Computer, Foreign Languages, and Health. The schedule for these classes will be established by an administrator, and it is very important that you adhere to the times. A librarian will see your students on a selected day, for an allotted time period. It is crucial to arrive and depart on time. He or she may only have a few minutes from the departure of one class until the arrival of another. It is very difficult to cover two classes at once and being late is not the best way to form a pleasant relationship. It is also important to keep the lines of communication open with each specialist. Here are some tips on maximizing the time your students spend at specials:

❖ At the beginning of a new chapter or unit, let the specialists know what your students will be studying. If you are studying weather, the music teacher may be able to do songs about weather or introduce instruments that sound like rain or thunder. The librarian may be able to read stories related to weather and pull out books that may interest the students for independent reading. The art teacher may do a project that focuses on weather. When instruction is supplemented in this manner, it becomes more meaningful for the students, making your objectives easier to achieve.

❖ Discuss behavior with the specialists. They may only see your class once a week, and it will make their time more productive if they know you will assist them with behavior issues.

❖ Always be on time. You may find some staff members who bring their class early and pick them up late. Do not follow this example and give the specialists a reason to be annoyed with you. Respect their schedule and the work they do.

❖   Send your students prepared. If they are going to the library and they need a pencil, be sure they each have a sharpened pencil and any books that need to be returned. This is a courtesy that specialists will appreciate.

Professional Services

Your school may have a Guidance Counselor, a Speech Therapist, Basic Skills Teachers, a Child Study Team, and other professionals that work with students individually. Whether they work full time in one building or split their time between several buildings, it is a good idea to get to know them. Their job is to assist students beyond what you are doing in the classroom. They are a wonderful resource if you are concerned about a student's progress, as they are highly trained in areas that you may not be. To get the most out of their services, try the following:

❖   If you have a student receiving these services, make it a point to discuss the student's progress with the provider. Keep abreast of improvements or additional difficulties the student may be facing.

❖   Discuss any changes you have noticed. Inform the team of any situation that may affect the student's progress in a certain area.

❖   Ask what you can do, in the classroom, to support their work.

❖   Always have the student ready on time. Their time is limited and waiting five minutes for a student to prepare is not fair to them or the student.

❖   If a student is absent, notify the provider as soon as possible. This free period may enable them to spend extra time with another student who would benefit by additional assistance.

Substitute Teachers

Some people assume a substitute will sit at a desk and read the paper while students complete crossword puzzles and quietly make it through the day. This is not an effective approach. A substitute teacher should be able to continue instruction and handle discipline issues that arise in the class. While you cannot control what a substitute does, you can see that they have everything they need to continue instruction. If you know you will be absent, use the opportunity to prepare your class. If you are unexpectedly absent, be sure your substitute is thoroughly prepared. The best way to ensure that this happens is to try the following:

❖ Keep your lesson plans updated, in a substitute folder, clearly marked, and in a convenient location. It is a good idea to let two or three teachers and the secretary know where you will keep it. While you can usually prepare for a substitute, there will be occasions when you will need to take off at the last minute. Whether it is a sudden illness or a family crisis, it will ease your mind to know that your substitute is prepared.

❖ Always keep a list of rules in your substitute folder.

❖ Ask the sub to leave a note regarding material covered and student behavior. Students behave better and accomplish more if they know that you have high expectations for them, even when you are absent.

❖ When you return, discuss the note with the class. Praise the positive and let them know negative reports are unacceptable.

❖ Be sure the substitute has plenty of work and clear instructions. Do not assign complicated activities. Remember, he or she is not familiar with the units you have been teaching.

❖ If you see the substitute when you return, thank him or her and request feedback. Would he or she like to share any suggestions with you? Was there enough work? Were the directions clear?

Crossing Guards and Bus Drivers

Finally, we must discuss the Crossing Guards and Bus Drivers. Even though you are not with your students as they walk to school or ride the buses, it is a good idea to let them know that you expect excellent behavior and will be checking with the crossing guards and bus drivers. This is a matter of safety as well as respect. The following should help you develop working relationships with the bus drivers and crossing guards:

❖ Introduce yourself to the crossing guards. Let them know that you are interested in the behavior of your students.

❖ Discuss appropriate behavior when riding the bus, waiting for the bus, and crossing the street.

❖ Let your students know that their behavior on the bus will be reported to you and ultimately, to their parents.

❖ If a safety issue arises, notify the principal and parents

In conclusion, the staff mentioned in this chapter perform various tasks and duties that support the work you will do in the classroom. Whether it is driving your students to school safely, preparing nutritious lunches, checking their vision, or talking them through a family crisis, each of these roles is vital to the success of your students. The key is to get to know these people, be respectful of their time, and be appreciative of their contributions. You will be able to establish positive relationships with all members of the school community by being considerate, courteous, and patient. It is well worth the time and the effort.

Chapter 3

Know What You Teach and
Teach What You Know

In a perfect world, all teachers would be experts in each subject they are required to teach. In reality, most teachers, especially at the elementary level, are expected to teach a variety of subjects. As a teacher, you must know the curriculum and the sequence of each subject you will be teaching throughout the school year.

The best way to become knowledgeable in your curriculum is to visit your school, the Superintendent's office, or the Board of Education office and obtain your own copies of the curriculum guides that pertain to your grade level. Curriculum guides are public information and anyone interested in looking at them or obtaining copies is permitted to do so. This information is not limited to educators, meaning that parents can (and will) know what you are (and are not) supposed to be teaching.

Just In Time

If you are lucky enough to have been hired at the beginning of the summer, get the curriculum guides as soon as possible and read them before the school year starts. This will provide you with a glimpse of how to map out the school year. Try to plan certain concepts at logical times of the school year. For example, if you are required to teach your class a Science unit on plants, you may decide to do that unit in the spring when planting and blooming usually occur. If your class is studying Native Americans as part of your Social Studies curriculum, you may want to wait until Thanksgiving and highlight the relationship between the Native Americans and the Pilgrims.

Better Late Than Never

If you are hired in late August or during the school year, take home the curriculum guides and read them cover-to-cover. It will be beneficial to know exactly what you are required to teach during the school year, as soon as possible. When reviewing the guides, note areas where you can overlap skills and concepts. For instance, if volcanoes and earthquakes are part of your Science curriculum and you are expected to teach your class how to write a research report as part of your Language Arts curriculum, combine the two ideas. While teaching your students about volcanoes and earthquakes, have them choose an area they wish to research and write a report about it. You can show them the steps involved in report writing while they are learning about volcanoes and earthquakes. Finally, have your students give oral presentations of their reports, and you will probably fulfill your requirements in the Speaking and Listening section of your Language Arts curriculum.

Spontaneously Structured?

Once you have mapped out your tentative plans for the year and you clearly understand your curriculum, it is important to stick to it. Keep in mind that there will be times when it is necessary to stray from your curriculum and do an isolated lesson on a different topic. If there is a presidential election during the school year, you will definitely want to take the opportunity to introduce the information to your class. You do not, however, want to spend the entire month of October preparing for the election and the entire month of November discussing the results. You also do not want to do an entire unit on France because you vacationed there and have great pictures to share. As it is, you will be struggling to complete everything that is required. In addition, the study of France may be part of the curriculum for another grade level. By introducing a unit of study that is not part of your curriculum, you could create tension between yourself and other teachers. It is also a good idea to check with other teachers before beginning a new book that you would like to read aloud to your class. It may be required text for the students in a higher grade and by reading it to your class, you may affect another teacher's instruction.

You Must Have A Hobby

It is beneficial to share your expertise with your students. For instance, if you love to do origami try to incorporate it into another unit of study. You could have the class make an origami animal and then write about it for a creative writing lesson. You could teach the students to make small boxes to store their math flashcards or make an origami penguin to supplement your science unit. If you are an avid reader, start a book club and hold a reading contest where students can earn small prizes for reading. If you are interested in geology, you can integrate a rock lesson into a science lesson about comparing objects or using observation skills. You could also do a math lesson with rocks during your measuring unit. There are many ways to include special areas of personal interest into your lessons without getting off the subject and possibly stepping on someone else's toes. You need to be creative and use your skills to apply the topic to an area of *your curriculum*.

Take A Deep Breath

As you plan the sequence of your units, you will want to cover as much of your curriculum as possible. Remember, however, that it is virtually impossible to cover all of the textbooks and every part of the curriculum. Keep your expectations realistic and accomplish as much as you can. Do your best to complete what the other teachers on your grade level have completed. The teachers in the next grade rely on you to teach the students specific skills, concepts, and material. If cursive writing is part of your curriculum and you rarely teach it, your students will be at a disadvantage when they reach the next grade. This is not fair to the children, as they will be behind their new classmates. Check with other teachers on your grade level, from time to time, to be sure that you are on track. See where they are in each subject, as this will enable you to gauge your progress and realistically achieve your curriculum goals.

Homework Headaches

During the school day, you will cover the majority of skills and concepts as classwork. To support the material introduced during class, homework is used as an extension. Be sure when assigning homework that it compliments the material that you are covering in class. Homework also keeps parents informed and enables them to observe their child's progress. Since some students will not receive assistance with their homework, be sure that all work assigned can be completed independently. This is an area where many children have an *unfair disadvantage.* Here are some tips and ideas to keep homework appropriate and productive for all:

❖   Since homework policies vary by school and grade, you should familiarize yourself with these policies before the year begins.

❖   Do not assign homework just for the sake of assigning it. Homework should be meaningful and an extension of classwork. Students need to know that homework is important and that their teacher will check it. If homework is not checked daily, they will not take it seriously. Also, if students know that another student will be checking their homework, they may not always do their best work. If you plan to have students check each other's work, do not share this information with them until the last minute.

❖   Be sensitive to extenuating circumstances. For example, do not assign a huge report due the day after Halloween. In addition, be understanding if a child has a family member who is ill or if they are going through a family crisis.

❖ Do not overlook the importance of holidays. For many families, a long weekend or religious holiday is a very special and hectic time. Be understanding and assign the absolute minimum if you must assign homework.

❖ Be consistent. Do not give 3 hours of homework on Monday and 20 minutes on Tuesday. If possible, set up a predictable schedule in a subject like Spelling. Assign the same homework on various days of the week. Parents will appreciate the routine and student confidence will increase as they master the assignments. The following is an example of a subject with fixed assignments.

Weekly Spelling Assignments

▤ Monday – Write the definition of each spelling word.

▤ Tuesday – Use each spelling word in a sentence.

▤ Wednesday – Write a funny story using all words.

▤ Thursday – Write each word 5 times. Study for test.

❖ Be Clear. It is important to walk students through an assignment, regardless of how simple it appears. If the class finds an assignment generally easy, a student who is struggling or confused may be apprehensive about asking questions. Explain everything! It's better to over-explain and model what is expected than to increase student anxiety with inadequate instruction.

Turn Lemons Into Lemonade

When a lesson makes a quick turn off the course you have carefully charted, relax. As a teacher, students will model your behavior and reaction to events and an effective teacher can turn almost anything into a learning experience. So go with the flow and accept interruptions, miscommunications, and missing materials and your students will observe valuable coping skills in addition to what you have planned.

During my first year as a teacher, I developed a unit on seeds and plants to use with my second grade class. I had researched the content of the unit and found that one of the best ways to show the parts of a seed and how plants grow is to use lima beans. The information I read suggested soaking the beans in water for 24 hours prior to the lesson. I remember reading that the beans would open easily so that the children could observe the baby plant inside.

Right before I left my classroom for the evening, I poured an entire bag of dried lima beans into a bowl of water and placed it on the back counter of the classroom. I planned to do the lesson the following day. Using the observations as an introduction to the unit, we would then plant the seeds and chart their growth. Not having much of a green thumb, my biggest concern was arriving to find a bowl full of wet lima beans.

The next morning, when I arrived, I was greeted by hundreds of lima beans, EVERYWHERE! They were stuck to the counter top, to the cabinets under the counter, to the sides of the bowl, all over the papers on the counter and carpet. One by one, hysterical teachers entered my room. I could feel my face turning redder and redder. Shortly after, the students started to arrive. They loved seeing the beans everywhere and began begging to do more experiments! In addition, they will surely never forget that dried beans expand when soaking in water. -LB

Chapter 4

A Place For Everything and
Everything In Its Place

Most new teachers never give much thought to the vast amounts of paperwork that are required throughout the year. Before the year even begins, however, the paperwork starts. You will be given a class list, permission slips, insurance forms, lunch applications, schedules, and a variety of other forms. Without a great organization system in place, it is very easy to misplace important documents. This chapter deals with the skill of organization and the benefit of having everything in its rightful place.

Two Copies Are Better Than One

One of the most important tools to achieve organization is the duplicate rule. As you receive important documents, make a copy and keep them together in a special file. This method of back up will prevent you from losing necessary paperwork and requesting additional copies.

In Arms Reach

Once the duplicate copy is in place, decide where the original will go. Whether it is a schedule, a bus list, or any information that you need to refer to frequently, keep it posted in an easy access area. Many teachers neatly hang important papers on the wall behind their desks. If this is not an option, make a bulletin board where the information will be attractively displayed.

> **Caution** - never *display* information that is sensitive to a student's abilities or needs, such as free lunch, speech therapy, or medical conditions.

Invest In A Binder

Before the paperwork descends upon you, be prepared. Set up a binder with a master sheet in the front. On this sheet, have a chart with a list of students' names and all papers they will be responsible to return. Above each form, write the date the form was distributed and check off the child's name as the forms are returned. Hole punch the forms and keep them in the binder for easy access. Keep a blank copy of each and use it as the first page of the section. If a student loses his or her form, a replacement will be ready for the copy machine. If a form is not returned and the deadline is approaching, send another form home in a sealed envelope. There is a good chance that the parents never saw the first form. If the form is still not returned, contact the parents by phone.

> *In the beginning of the school year, the students will be bombarded with forms that must be signed by their parents and returned. Regardless of the importance you place upon returning these items, you will have several students who will continually forget to bring them back.*
>
> *During my first year, I realized how hard it would be to have 26 children return their forms on time. I decided to approach the situation using positive reinforcement. Each child decorated a folder that contained each form and a list of the forms they were responsible for returning. On the outside of the folder was a permission slip to walk to a nearby park for a Bubble Experiment. I then explained that every student who returned the folder, with all items signed, would be able to participate.*

> *To make the event more interesting, I found a copy of the recipe for homemade bubbles. The students did an experiment to compare store-bought bubbles versus homemade bubbles. I gave the students 3 days to return the forms. The following morning, every folder was returned and we reviewed the procedures for an experiment. By keeping the forms organized in a special folder and providing an age-appropriate incentive, the children became responsible for the documents. It was also a great way to introduce science experiments to second graders. -LW*

For many schools, the lunch aid form is one of the most important. In low-income districts, this form determines the amount of aid a school receives. Explain to the class that this form must be returned and offer a class treat when all forms are returned. Something as simple as a game of kickball or an extra in-class art period may be enough incentive to ensure a speedy return.

Permission slips are another extremely important item. They are more than permission for a student to take a walk or go on a trip. These slips may save your school, your principal, and yourself from an enormous lawsuit. Most schools have a walking slip which permits students to take walks outside of the building. Some walking permission slips cover all walks for the school year, others only cover an individual trip, requiring a new slip for each outing. While a simple walk may not sound dangerous, it could be. Do not allow students to participate in any activity requiring parental permission, if they do not have it in writing. A student, upset because of a forgotten permission slip, may beg you to call his or her parents and secure verbal permission. This could become a slippery slope. If the walk is uneventful, there would not be a problem. If the unthinkable happens and a student is injured and you do not have a signed permission slip, the parent may not admit to giving permission. Take permission slips seriously to avoid these issues.

Incomplete Information Alert

During the first week of school, parents will probably be required to fill out an information form. This form will have the student's address, contact information, medical conditions, and parents' employers. As the forms are returned, be sure they are completely filled out. Parents are busy and may be signing a stack of papers for several children, thus signing this important form without providing the necessary information. If you do not catch this error, you will not be able to contact the family in the event of an emergency. This form is usually forwarded to the nurse's office or the main office. If that is the case, be sure to copy importnat imformation before submitting forms.

Individual Student Records

Another great way to keep accurate records of student progress is to maintain a binder with a section for each student. This is a valuable tool for comparing progress over a period of time and noting improvements and problems that develop. Remember, this is a professional record and should be written in an objective manner. Notes should never be mean or written in the heat of frustration. The most effective method is to write the facts of an incident and the results. Do not include your opinion or commentary in writing. Constantly update each student and include measures taken by the student or the family.

Check It Once, Check It Twice

During your first year, when sending home a letter that may cause a negative reaction on the part of the parent, it is wise to have your principal look it over. This serves two purposes. The principal will approve a written correspondence while becoming familiar with a situation that may eventually be brought to his or her attention. Use your discretion when having a principal review letters. A simple note stating that a student had a great day, should not require a review, unless stipulated by policy.

Keeping Records

As a teacher, one of the most important things you will do is keep records. You will record academic progress, social progress, and behavior. The following are reasons you should maintain impeccable records of everything you do:

❖ The objective of educating is to teach a group of children a prescribed amount of material, based upon the curriculum, during the course of a school year. Records do not tell the whole story, but they give teachers an idea of student progress. They help a teacher evaluate competency in the skill or a need for additional instruction.

❖ Homework, whether given in large or small doses, needs to be recorded. This is an extension of what the class is learning; therefore, it is vital to keep track of completed assignments. Since parents are the main contact when it comes to homework, you need to have specific information if you call a parent regarding homework. It would be unprofessional to casually mention that, during the last month, some assignments were missing or incomplete. You should never wait a month to notify a parent of missing or incomplete assignments. When you do contact a parent, you should be able to tell them which assignments you are referring to and the dates these assignments were given.

❖ Classwork, as with homework, should also be recorded. For many assignments, a simple check mark will be sufficient, for others, you will assign a grade. Either way, you will want to keep accurate records, which should include participation or lack thereof.

❖ You will be happy that your records are impeccable when parents show up, unannounced, and request a conference. It is difficult to have the data parents are looking for on the tip of your tongue. By referring to your records, you will appear diligent and seriously interested in helping their child.

❖ If a student is having a problem, a parent may take your word for it or may resist and demand documentation. For this reason, you must be able to support any statements you make, positive or negative. In addition to grades and check marks, take the time to record anecdotal notes. Whether it is a paragraph or a few words, it will enable you to speak intelligently about student progress and add relevant suggestions.

❖ When a student experiences difficulties in an academic area, it is wise to refer a student for further evaluation, via a Child Study Team. This generally requires a conference and parental permission. In order to obtain that permission, you should present all data that supports your request. Communication with the parents needs to be ongoing and should occur well before a student requires this type of evaluation. The records you keep will be an integral part of the evaluation process.

❖ When a student experiences behavioral difficulties, records of the incidents are vital in addressing the situation and finding a solution. Behavioral problems are often the result of many factors and are affected by a combination of circumstances. Recording the offense, time of day, other students involved, and consequence for the action will help determine the cause or a pattern. This information will also determine if the student requires additional testing, medication, or intervention.

Lesson Plans

Lesson Plans are another form of record keeping. Your lesson plans are the guide you follow throughout the day. They are more than an outline of *what you will do*. They provide scope and sequence and the length of time you will spend on a specific chapter or unit. You must remember, however, they are only a guide. It is more important to record *what you have accomplished* than to feel that you must complete everything you have written down. Keep notes on progress and understand that many things will impact your well-thought-out lesson plans. This list ranges from fire drills to assemblies to snow days to students needing extra time on a particular concept. By keeping honest, accurate lesson plans, you will be able to adjust to your students' needs.

I Know There's A Desk Around Here Somewhere

When your room is organized, labeled, and decorated it is time to think smaller. It is time to think about your desk. You cannot imagine how easy it is to lose a clean desk under a mountain of papers. It can literally happen in minutes. Invest in some office supplies, such as stackable trays, paper clip organizers, two or three pen/pencil holders, etc. Keep your teachers' guides and resource materials very close to your desk. Keep your attendance/grade book in a place that is easy to reach. When a fire drill is executed, you must immediately exit the building and take roll. There will not be an opportunity to start digging through the paper mountain to locate your attendance book.

In Lieu Of A Scheduling Secretary

In your attendance book, keep a schedule of all children who leave your room at a regularly scheduled time, whether it is for supplemental instruction, to take medicine, or to meet with a counselor. It is difficult to keep so many schedules stored in your head, and a schedule will help you to have all of this information accessible.

Make a habit of recording all dates as you receive them. If eye exams are scheduled for the 14th at 11:00 a.m., write it down. If there is an assembly on the 26th at 2:00 p.m., write it down. When you plan your weekly lessons, always refer to your calendar to ensure you are not forgetting any events. Your principal and colleagues will not appreciate your class arriving late to an event to which you were previously notified.

On Your Mark, Get Set, Teach!

Organization may sound trivial compared to curriculum and classroom management, but effective organization will impact all areas of teaching. It takes very little effort to organize, but it can take weeks to re-organize. Surely, you can think of better ways to spend your time!

Chapter 5

Walk A Mile In Their Shoes or
Spend A Moment In Their Desks

From the moment you are hired, your classroom becomes a second home for you and *your students*. You will spend an enormous amount of time in the school, but the majority of your time will be spent in your classroom. It will be well worth the effort to take your time and thoroughly plan the décor and layout of your room. Keep the following items in mind when you plan your own classroom.

Where Is The Front Of The Room?

First, examine your room from all angles. Take note of the location of windows, chalkboards, and entrances. Often times, the front of the room is established on account of the boards. While there is no rule designating the chalkboard as the front of the room, it is convenient to have your students facing the board. Older children can generally turn around without incident; however, you may find that having younger students turn around is a daunting task. You will no doubt conduct many of your lessons with the chalkboard as the main focal point. Be sure that the students can see the board clearly and are comfortable. Students that must twist and turn in their seats will become quite fidgety. Fidgety students tend to become disruptive, distracting themselves and those around them.

Opportunity Isn't The Only Thing That Knocks

Another consideration for your classroom will be the door. Children seated near or facing the door will incur constant distractions when the door is open. The air circulation resulting from an open door may not be worth the noise and distractions that may result. A tall fan and open windows may be a better solution if the temperature becomes uncomfortable. If space issues require that a portion of students be seated near the doors, be selective with the students you choose.

A Wonderful Desk With A View

Windows can be another contributing factor to distractions. Your room may have a full wall of windows or no windows at all. They may face an uneventful field or a busy street. It is important to assess the role the windows will play in your instruction. If your windows face the front of the building, the playground, or the parking lot, it will be easy for your students to become distracted. Be sure that you have blinds, shades, or curtains to obstruct the view. Keep them closed when the areas in view are active. If your windows provide no entertainment whatsoever, keep them decorated with content-driven decorations. Capitalize on the fact that students will be drawn to the window when they are tired, bored, or interested in the weather. Enhance their view with decorations that will help them learn or pique their interest, *even when they daydream.*

Table For One

Placement of seats and assignment of children to those seats are two of the most significant factors affecting student behavior. Group seating can work beautifully if the right students are grouped together. Before you can select the right students, you will need to 'know' your students; therefore, you may opt for a more conservative seating arrangement for the first week. While columns and rows do not scream excitement and creativity, they will provide you with an opportunity to get to know students before arranging desks in pairs, trios, or groups.

Try One On For Size

Every time you rearrange the seats in your room, make it a point to sit in each desk for a moment. Do this at the end of the day or early in the morning and observe how the desk feels. Ask yourself the following questions:

❖ What will your students be looking at?

❖ Are there any significant distractions that will affect any seats?

❖ Is there enough room for students to maneuver in and out without disturbing other students?

❖ Does each seat have a clear view of the board?

The only way to really answer these questions is to sit in each desk. This is similar to parents of toddlers crawling around to see the view from a small child's level. You will see what your students see, and this is a valuable perspective.

> *From the first day of school, students become preoccupied with where they will be sitting and who they will be sitting near. I learned that seating arrangements can be a tremendous tool for classroom management and instruction.*
>
> *When I was teaching fourth grade one year, I soon realized that five students were non-readers and several students were significantly below grade level. Few of these students participated and several were the cause of classroom disruptions.*

> *If you think about it, however, can you blame them? They did not understand what was going on and were unable to complete an assignment on their own. Quite simply, they were bored and frustrated.*
>
> *I decided to rely on the old adage, opposites attract. I paired students who performed well with students who were having tremendous difficulties. I carefully observed their interaction and noticed a wonderful transformation. Within a week, the students who were doing well were explaining concepts to their peers. The students who were having difficulties rose to the occasion and gained much needed confidence. Discipline issues dramatically decreased and time on task increased. The most impressive benefit was watching children who might have never become friends, develop a bond, working as a team. -LW*

The Pitter Patter Of Little Feet

If your classroom floor is not carpeted, you may want to place tennis balls on the bottom of the chairs. This will help keep the movements of your class from disturbing the classes nearby or beneath you. With your principal's permission, you may request that parents send in tennis balls if they can. Since each student only needs four, be sure to tell the parents to send no more than four, but to let you know if they have extra for a student who may not bring any. Otherwise, you will have more tennis balls than the U.S. Open! (Carefully make two cuts in the top of each ball and slide onto the bottom of each chair leg.)

It Must Be The Maid's Day Off

Maintain a clean and clutter-free classroom. It will be difficult for you to teach and your students to learn if the room is a mess. With an average of two dozen students plus yourself, it is easy for a room to become messy. When you begin to set up your room in the summer, sift through everything that was left behind. Discard anything that you know you will not use. Look at other classrooms for ideas on creative storage. Many teachers find that built in shelves with a slot for each student work well to limit the papers that accumulate. If you do not have built in shelves, you can make similar items yourself with boxes that have been decorated. Keep student paper and extra pencils in a spot that is easy to reach. Keep your class library in order. Find a place for everything and use labels so the children will know where everything is stored. If you organize and label your room prior to the first day of school, the students will be more apt to keep the environment orderly and you will eliminate the unnecessary stress caused by chaos.

Help Wanted

Assign weekly helpers to keep the room tidy. This is a shared space and the effort required to maintain order should also be shared. A chart with each job and a hook or velcro to affix the name of the student responsible will serve as a reminder that this is a group effort. The following are examples of standard jobs that may be rotated among the students and completed at the end of the day:

- ❖ Clean and wash the boards.
- ❖ Straighten the rows of seats.
- ❖ Collect garbage from students.
- ❖ Empty the pencil sharpener.
- ❖ Pick up debris from the floor.
- ❖ Empty the garbage.
- ❖ Water the plants.

Of course, these may not apply to your classroom and there may be other jobs that you find necessary. Use jobs that will be meaningful to your classroom and teach students that this is a team activity.

Interior Design 101

There are thousands of resources available on how to decorate a classroom. A well decorated room will have bright visuals and engaging content increasing the aesthetic value. Students will be more productive in a colorful environment. Many students are visual learners and bulletin boards, posters, and mobiles create a sense of learning. Another reason is again, capitalizing on daydreamers. At various points throughout the day, students' eyes will wander around the room. Have your students stare at a poster of the solar system or the parts of a bug's body as opposed to a blank wall. You will find that they are learning even when they are off task.

Decorating your room is a wonderful way to motivate your students to learn, but there is one catch. You need to change your decorations frequently. Not all of them, but the ones that pertain to the units being studied or the time of year. If you are studying bugs, you may have a bug bulletin board and bug posters scattered around the room. When the unit is completed and you switch to plants, be sure to change your bulletin board and decorations. They are great visual aids and help improve student retention of material. By changing the room frequently, you will avoid having your classroom become boring and uninspiring.

Never underestimate the value of decorating your classroom. The aesthetics of a student's surroundings can play an important role in motivation and achievement. You will spend an enormous amount of time in your classroom and you should strive to create a neat, welcoming environment. Add little touches from home, pictures, and conversation pieces. It may sound trivial, but as the year progresses, you will understand how many little factors combine to create a total learning atmosphere.

Years ago, teachers would use stencils to trace letters of the alphabet for their bulletin boards, carefully cutting out each letter. Overhead projectors were used to project images on posterboard, to be traced, colored, and cut. Worksheets were handwritten or created with ditto masters and run off on mimeograph machines.

Thankfully, technology has reached the point where homemade decorations are not a necessity. If you have not had the opportunity to visit your local teacher supply store or peruse an educational supply catalog, you are in for a treat. Almost anything you can imagine is available and the time you will save and use to plan better lessons will be well worth the cost of the items. In Chapter 15, we provide a comprehensive selection of resources, including free items for teachers, stores, catalogs, and websites.

Tip: Laminate the materials that you use in your room. Air, sun, and moisture take a toll on these posters and you want to get as much use out of them as possible.

The Walls of Fame

Be sure to display student work around the room. Students love the praise and attention they receive when they accomplish a goal. Displaying their work shows them that you have noticed. There are bulletin board sets that allow you to display the names of each student in a very creative manner. One example is a large tree that comes with 36 apples. You can use punch out letters to title the board, perhaps saying *Mrs. Jones' New Crop*, and write each student's name on the apples provided. You can continually change the tree to reflect the different seasons by replacing the apples with fall leaves, winter snowflakes, or spring raindrops.

Keep Your Current Events Current

Maintain a current events bulletin board. This is a fantastic way to broaden your students' horizons while relating current events to topics being studied. It is also an opportunity for students to bring in articles from the newspaper that they would like to post and discuss with the class. This is a wonderful activity for the end of the day, when you will want the class to wind down. This makes for a calm clean up period and dismissal. Remember, a current events bulletin board is only as good as it is current. Make an effort to continually refresh the content.

Chapter 6

Please Report
To The Principal's Office

The words, "Report to the Principal's office," probably sent chills down your spine when you were a student. Unfortunately, for a new teacher, you may still get chills. Since your childhood, you have been in awe of *the principal* and now this powerful person is *your boss!* Theoretically, the relationship you establish with your principal should be one of support and guidance. The good news is that most principals are wonderful people who appreciate the efforts of their staff and enjoy working with children. They set the tone for the building and you can learn from their experience. Of course, there are exceptions to every rule. You may find that your principal is neither a people person nor particularly fond of children. It happens. This chapter will provide pointers for working with your principal, wonderful or not so wonderful.

Before the school year begins, you will likely have opportunities to get to know your principal. When the students are not in the building, the adults have more time and opportunity to get to know one another. In a small school, there may be significantly more interaction with your principal, than in a large school. Keep your conversations friendly and professional. This is not the time to try out a new joke. Assess your principal's personality. Is he or she casual or uptight? Quiet or talkative? Serious or charming? Intimidating or welcoming?

I was hired by a principal that was easy to speak with and enthusiastic to have a fresh new teacher in his school. Then I found out he was retiring before the school year would start. Shortly after, I received a phone call from the school secretary, asking me to come in for a meeting with the new principal.

Unfortunately, this meeting wasn't nearly as enjoyable as my meeting with the newly-retired principal. There was no small talk, no coffee, and no smile. I immediately knew that he would not have hired me. How did I know? He told me. That's right, he came out and admitted that I would never have been selected by him. At that point I wasn't sure if I should be happy that I was hired just in time or terrified because my new boss hated me!

As a new principal, he had planned to hire teachers with classroom experience and a Masters Degree. I had neither. Besides stating his displeasure, he went on to tell me that he would be in my room everyday, observing my performance and waiting for mistakes. He made it clear that he expected the same from me as he did from the veteran teachers. I knew I would be under the magnifying glass and had little margin for error.

I went home, slightly shaken, but determined to prove myself. As the year began, he noticed my efforts and began to commend me on my performance. Parents, who were also apprehensive about a new teacher, were pleased and shared their feelings with him. By the end of the first month, I was no longer nervous. - LW

Middle School and High School Teachers

On the middle school and high school level, you will probably deal more with the head of your department. A department head will be able to guide your instruction and will be the person to whom you bring your concerns to and will be much more involved in your daily activities. Use the same suggestions below to form a positive relationship with them:

Strategies

Whether you are teaching pre-school or calculus, building a working relationship with your principal is vital. Try the following ideas to lay the ground work for positive interactions.

Be Professional

Conduct yourself as a competent professional. The school is a work environment, and you want your principal to have confidence in your abilities. Remember, that you are part of a team and that requires give and take. *Assist whenever possible; accept assistance graciously.*

Be An Asset

Work hard to be an asset to the school, not a liability. As a new teacher, your main priority should be learning every aspect of your job. Be conservative in your decision-making. This is not the time to take risks. When in doubt, err on the side of caution.

Be Yourself

During your first year of teaching, you will hardly have time to invent and maintain a new personality. Principals are accustomed to working with a wide variety of personalities, including teachers, students, and parents. The majority of principals are able to separate professional qualities from personal preferences.

Be Realistic

Have realistic expectations. Do not expect your principal to spend hours molding your raw teaching ability. The reality is, principals are extremely busy. Their responsibilities are endless. They are liable for every student, the actions of their staff, budgets, and at least a hundred other items. If it seems as though your principal is paying little attention to you, this is not necessarily cause for alarm. On the contrary, your principal may be very confident with your abilities and impressed by your competence.

Be Clear

Do not try to read your principal's mind. If you need specific information, do not try to guess what your principal would say. By the same token, do not read too much into non-verbal cues. If your principal passes you in the hall without looking up, do not take it personally. Chances are, he or she would not remember the incident.

Beware Of Being The Principal's Pet

Avoid being the principal's pet. It is one thing to be a team player, it is quite another to become the favorite teacher. As a new teacher, this is a role you want to avoid. There is no easier way to bring the scrutiny of every staff member your way, than to become the principal's pet.

Be Conscientious

Do what is expected of you. Simple things, such as arriving on time, dressing professionally, and maintaining effective classroom management, will be noticed. The best thing you can do is to blend into the woodwork and become one less thing for a principal to worry about.

Be Independent

Do not make a habit of constantly reporting to your principal. You may feel the desire to share all of the wonderful things you do with your students. Follow your principal's lead. You will find yourself casually observed much more than you think. If not, continue to provide the highest level of instruction and eventually, it will be noticed.

Agree To Disagree

Unfortunately, you may be faced with a situation where, regardless of your efforts, you cannot reach common ground. You must keep in mind that principals are people, with their own personalities, likes, and dislikes. While the majority of principals are able to separate their feelings, there are exceptions. If you find that the relationship between you and your principal is strained, take steps to address the situation.

Examine your behavior

- ❖ Have you followed all the rules?

- ❖ When your principal observes you in the class room, is your class on task?

- ❖ When you are observed in the hallways, is your class quiet and orderly?

- ❖ Have you made negative statements regarding the principal?

- ❖ Have you made an effort to get along with the staff?

Be honest as you answer these questions. If you have a mentor or are close with a member of your grade level unit, you may ask if he or she has noticed anything. Do not go into detail, just general questions.

Perhaps your principal is going through a family crisis that only veteran staff members would know about. Perhaps this is just your principal's personality and your colleagues will be able to ease your mind that it is not *just you*.

Be Observant

Pay special attention to your interactions and look for clues that may help you resolve matters. Does it seem like every time you are late, your principal is annoyed? If the answer is yes, **STOP BEING LATE.**

Determine The Nature Of The Problem

Is the situation one of neglect? Do you feel that your principal ignores your accomplishments or requests for assistance? As mentioned before, a principal is extremely busy, and as a result, no contact is often good news. Your principal may also have a laid back style. Try to observe his or her interactions with other staff members. Is the situation confrontational or hostile? Have you been written up for minor infractions and feel that you are being singled out? If the answer is yes, you will want to address this situation as soon as possible. Begin by documenting everything you do, as keeping written records is often your best defense.

When you have done your best to improve the situation, it may be time to accept the fact that, for whatever reasons, your principal does not like you. Even though this is your boss, it is not the end of the world. As long as you do your job and do it well, you should not have a problem. Continue to be cordial, professional, and open to a change for the better, if it should occur. If the situation has deteriorated to the point where you are being written up or called in for reprimands, you need to protect yourself. If you belong to an education association or union, you should do the following:

Call In The Cavalry

If you are part of a union, contact a representative. You may be advised to consult with your building representative; however, you should give this extensive thought and consider the following:

- ❖ Do you want to place someone from your building in the center of this situation? Do you trust the representative from your building? Are you concerned that the details will be shared with the entire staff? Keep in mind, that you always have the option, to secure a representative from outside of your building.

- ❖ In serious situations, do not agree to meet your principal without union representation. Simply request the union representative, of *your choice,* to represent you.

- ❖ Attend meetings with documentation and a pad for notes.

- ❖ Do not speak unless you have discussed the matter with your representative.

- ❖ Remain calm and professional. Refrain from sighing, rolling your eyes, or showing your distaste.

- ❖ Let your representative represent you; they know your rights.

On A More Positive Note

As the school year progresses, you should feel more comfortable interacting with your principal. Regardless of personality type, you will learn what to expect, what his or her priorities are, and how to safely navigate through this new relationship. A principal is your boss and as a new teacher, you should do whatever you can to ensure that this relationship thrives. The best way to ensure its success is to be the best teacher you can be. When all is said and done, your principal will judge you by your ability to teach.

Chapter 7

A Diamond In The Rough

Although every chapter in this book is important, the relationships you establish with the parents of your students is vital to a successful teaching career. This relationship is similar to a diamond in the rough and it is up to you, as the teacher, to transform it into a valuable partnership. Without your effort, you will never see its true beauty or potential. The first thing to keep in mind is that you cannot please everyone. For reasons, often beyond your control, you will encounter parents that find fault with everything you do. The good news is that the majority of parents you deal with will be kind, helpful, and supportive. They will share a common goal with you, the education of their children. To make the most of the relationship with your students' parents, follow these steps:

Respect

Give respect and get respect. The best way to do this is to address parents formally, by their surnames. It establishes a professional relationship when you call a parent and say, "Hello Mrs. Smith, this is Mrs. Jones, calling about John..." as opposed to, " Hi Karen, this is Mary calling to talk to you about John." This may feel awkward, at first, for someone who has just graduated from college or for someone who is younger than many of the parents they are dealing with. However, there is a certain level of respect that naturally develops when such a simple expectation is in place.

Partnership

View your relationship with the parents as a partnership. The goal is to have the parents on *your* side. If parents see that you want to help their children learn and grow to their fullest potential, they will be on your side and you will be able to accomplish more. Parents will be more apt to follow through with homework assignments and support your disciplinary actions. They will also trust your judgment and advice when problems or situations arise.

Open Door Policy

Have an "Open-Door Policy." At Back-to-School Night or in a letter sent in the beginning of the school year, tell parents "your door is always open." Encourage them to keep the lines of communication open and follow through. That way, if a child is going through a difficult time, you can contact the parent and resolve the situation before it escalates. Refrain, however, from giving your home number to parents. If you will be calling parents from home, consider having your phone number blocked or a caller identification operating to avoid calls at all hours.

Be Realistic

Be realistic and set realistic goals. Parents are not going to like you very much if you assign a detailed project over winter break. Look at the calendar and be sensitive to holidays when assigning due dates. Plan your projects so that they are not all due at the same time. Whenever possible allow the students to complete parts of the project in class. Allow students to work at lunch or at recess, if permitted by the principal. Acknowledge the hectic schedules and pressures that most parents are under and they will appreciate it.

Honesty

Always be honest and keep parents informed. This sounds really simple but can be difficult to put into practice. Unfortunately, there will be children in your class that are having some trouble and are not learning certain concepts. The best thing you can do for these children is to tell the parent right away. By being honest, you can work together and help the child. Remember that this is not a reflection of you or your teaching ability. Children develop at very different rates in all areas. If you are up-front with parents, they will trust you and support you. Telling a parent news that may be upsetting is extremely uncomfortable and you may be tempted to ease their worry and minimize the problems. This can hurt the relationship in the long run. As upsetting as it may be, parents need to know the facts to successfully help their child, and it is your job to suggest solutions, not to mislead or provide false hope. Once they accept the situation, they will appreciate your candor. If they never accept it and the relationship is damaged, you have still done the right thing.

Offer Extra Help

Offer extra help opportunities. By offering extra help time either before school, during lunch or recess, or after school, parents will believe that you care about their children a great deal. First check with your principal or colleagues, to be sure that this is acceptable. Let parents know the times you will be available.

Volunteers

Enlist volunteers. Whether it is during class parties, field trips, art projects, or writing exercises, ask for parent volunteers. Again, check with your principal before making any arrangements. Parents *love* to see what their children are doing and how they behave during school. By involving them in their child's education, they feel important and you get some assistance in the classroom. Once parents see you in action, they will appreciate you and all the wonderful things you do for their children.

Keep Records

As mentioned in Chapter 4, keep a list of any parent conferences and phone call dates in your plan book. Doing so throughout the school year will be beneficial for many reasons. First, and most importantly, it will keep you better organized. You will be able to remind the parent, as well as yourself, of when and how many times you have discussed a child. Second, it is necessary when a child will be referred to the Child Study Team. In that case, the team will find it helpful to know how often you have contacted the parent to discuss the child. Finally, it is a subtle way to show your principal the effort you put forth to keep the parents involved.

> One important note: do not make any notes about student behaviors or actions in your plan book. Many people, including your principal and substitute teachers will have access to your plan book, and this is not the forum for private information about a student. Keep a separate folder with anecdotal notes regarding student concerns, behaviors, and issues pertaining to your students.

Classroom Parents

If possible, select a class parent to be the contact person for other parent volunteers. Depending upon your school, you may be fortunate enough to have many helpers or you may not be able to enlist one. If you do have volunteers, it may be difficult to deal with a group of 10 parents. In that case, it is best to choose a contact volunteer, requiring you to only call one parent to set up parties, picnics, and class trips. Always try to select a parent that seems to be well organized and wants to be involved. Avoid choosing a parent that is currently the contact person in other classes. Pick a person that you feel comfortable with, as that person will spend a great deal of time in your room.

Flexibility

Remember that each child is unique and special and so is each parent. You may have to make a special arrangement for some parent conferences due to work schedules or business trips. Be as flexible as you can, without rearranging your entire conference schedule. Parents will appreciate your efforts to accommodate them.

> *During my first year teaching, a student came into school very upset. He told me that his parents were going away and would have to miss Back-To-School Night. We had been preparing things in our classroom and the students were very excited. I called his parents and rearranged my schedule. We set up an afternoon when his parents could visit the classroom and see all of his work. He waited all week for that day to come and when it did, his smile lit up the room. A few years later, his parents commented to me that they would never forget how special I made their son feel. You may never know the impact of a small act of kindness, but as a teacher, your kindness is rarely forgotten. - LB*

Common Goals

The education of a student is the responsibility of both the family and the school. In order for students to maximize their learning potential, both parties must be effective. The relationship you will establish with parents is a partnership with common goals. Do whatever it takes to get the parents on board. If a parent is difficult, try harder. Remember, you are not doing it for the parent, you are doing it for the student and you will be surprised by how many parents you win over.

The amount of parental support you receive will greatly depend upon your district. As an inner city teacher, I was accustomed to having little parental support. While I was fortunate to have a few parents each year, who wanted to volunteer, the majority of parents were not involved. I decided, with my principal's permission, to encourage their participation with various events every month and contacted parents with transportation to pick up interested parents without a car.

The first few events had a sparse turn out, but then something wonderful occurred. The students went home and told how exciting it was to have parents in the room. Before I knew it, our events drew a large crowd. Whether we made ice cream or walked to the firehouse, we invited parents and they came.

Since many students lived with grandparents, aunts or uncles, they were Family Days and any family member was invited. Attendance at PTA meetings may have been down, but classroom attendance, which was more important to the students, was up. -LW

Chapter 8

A Penny For Their Thoughts

Imagine being able to know what your students are thinking. Such information would surely be worth more than a penny; it would be priceless. Knowing each student as an individual is clearly one of the most important aspects of the teaching profession. In order to effectively teach your class, you must first take the time to reach each and every one of your students. The best way to know your students is by speaking *with* them. Find out what they like to do after school or on the weekends. Ask about favorite foods, movies, books, and colors. Discuss fads, sporting events, music groups, and animals. Simply take the time to have a conversation with your class whether it is 5 minutes before lunch or first thing in the morning a few times a week.

To do this with younger students, gather them, if possible, on a rug or on mats and tell them you will talk for 5 minutes. Because smaller children are easily drawn off the subject, remind them of what you will be discussing with a picture or word on the board or on chart paper. Although most children will wish to do all the talking for the 5 minutes, try to keep the conversation moving and remind them that you would like to hear from everyone. If time runs out, be sure to get back to the group and hear from each student before the end of the day. A good way to hurt their feelings is to ignore what they have to say or forget "their turn."

Getting to know each student requires significant effort but is worth the time. Invest the time in your students and the rewards will be immeasurable. Some students will be very easy to get to know and understand, others will require much more effort. Keep in mind that these may be the students who will appreciate your efforts the most. There are many ways to accomplish this task, both before and after the school year begins.

Before The School Year Begins

Know Your Students' Histories

Take the time to read through each child's portfolio or permanent record folder. Use the information as a guide, not to pass judgment. There may be pertinent information included in the folders that can help you understand a child even more. In addition, if the child has an I.E.P. (Individualized Educational Plan) make time to read it, from start to finish, so that you are fully aware of the contents.

Speak To Others

Speak to the school nurse, previous teachers, and special area teachers. If a child has a history of problems, try to talk to as many teachers as possible to develop strategies and start the new year on the right foot. Do not participate in gossip about a student. If someone has very few positive things to say about a particular student, politely listen and form your own opinions.

Know Your Students' Communities

Before the school year begins, take a few minutes, when you are busy setting up your classroom, to drive around the town or city. It is a great way to see where your students are coming from and understand their community.

Once The School Year Starts

Peer Interviews

Have each child interview another child and share it with the class. Set up pairs that do not already know one another well. It is as important for the students to know each other as it is for you to know them. Interviews are a fun way to bring students, who may not normally be drawn to each other, together.

Weekly Sharing Sessions

Have a weekly sharing session. Assign a topic and allow students to bring in items from home such as a favorite book or picture. Avoid having students bring in their favorite toys because this could leave some children feeling underprivileged.

Pair and Share

If time does not permit a whole class sharing session, pair your students and give them two minutes to share. For the first minute, one student speaks without interruption, followed by the other. After the two minutes, the partners report to the group.

KWL Chart

Use a KWL Chart. This strategy is used to gain knowledge about what your students know before beginning a unit or new concept, as well as after the unit is completed. The K stands for what the students KNOW. The W stands for what the students WANT to know. The L stands for what the class has LEARNED. Before formally introducing your new unit or concept, have a brainstorming session with the class and record the information on chart paper.

If you are starting a unit on dinosaurs, you would ask the students what they KNOW about dinosaurs. Then you would ask the students what they WANT to know about dinosaurs. Record all responses on the paper, even if the statements are incorrect. Keep the information you recorded until you finish teaching the unit. Once the unit is completed, have one more brainstorming session with the students and ask them what they have LEARNED about dinosaurs.

Take out the first two charts and compare them to the last one. You and your students will enjoy correcting their incorrect statements and see how much they have learned. It is a fun and interesting way to find out how much information, correct and incorrect, your students already have about a given subject.

Concentrate on Self-Esteem

Do a Self-Esteem unit. There are many units available that focus on the student as unique and special and celebrate the differences among all students. They usually include some type of "All About Me" paper for the student to complete. They also have interview sheets for the students to bring home and use with other family members.

Three Nice Things A Day

Say something nice to three students a day. Whether you comment on a nice hair-style, a bright smile, or an extra neat handwriting paper, it is important for individual students to feel special as often as possible. Try not to comment on only new clothes or sneakers since all children will not be able to afford the nicest items.

Role-play

Set up cooperative groups in your class. Provide each group with a topic that is age and grade appropriate, such as a problem on the playground. Allow each group a chance to act out how they would solve the problem. Encourage the class to discuss each group's response and provide feedback. Be sure, however, to model appropriate types of criticism. Students should know that negative feedback is acceptable, but personal attacks on other students, name calling, and teasing are not.

Puppet Shows

For younger students, use a puppet. They love to talk to and play with puppets. If you are looking for a new way to motivate your class, a puppet is perfect. Give the puppet a name and change your voice when you are pretending to be the puppet. Talk to the puppet as if it were another student in your class. Invite the class to do the same. Use the puppet when a situation arises, such as one student taking another student's pencil. The class will enjoy the lesson and get the message, too.

Let Your Students Get To Know You

It is just as important for the students to get to know you as it is for you to get to know them. Your students will trust you even more if they feel that you are human and that they can relate to you. **This does not mean that you should tell them where you go to happy hour or if you have any tattoos**. It is certainly appropriate to share your favorite baseball team, favorite food, the type of music you enjoy, or your favorite books. Keep in mind, however, that your word will be highly regarded by most students. They will love to hear real stories from when you were in school or about your family. Whenever possible, try to incorporate these topics into your discussions. **Under no circumstances, however, should you tell stories that are inappropriate or encourage students to do anything deemed dangerous.**

Understand Learning Styles

Once you get to know the different personalities of the students in your class, it is important to understand each learning style. This will allow you to individualize instruction to address each student's needs. There are three basic types of learning styles; however, a student can be a combination of two styles.

❖ **Visual Learners**

A visual learner learns best when information is presented visually on the board, on chart paper or in a book.

❖ **Auditory Learners**

An auditory learner easily processes information given orally.

❖ **Kinesthetic Learners**

A kinesthetic learner needs to use his/her body movements to internalize what he/she has learned and will benefit from tracing words in sand, using tactile games, and writing words in the air.

Determining Learning Styles

There are two ways to determine the learning styles of the students in your class: by observation and by simply asking the students questions that will help you determine their natural preferences.

❖ **Observation**

Through observation you can determine how your students prefer to learn. For example, if a student excels in math with a specific concept because you usually write the problems on the board, but has trouble when asked to do the problem orally or using mental math, he or she may be a visual learner. Take notes during the first weeks of school to determine patterns of learning styles. Adapt your lessons so that they meet the needs of your students. When introducing a new concept, use the three methods as often as possible to reach each student.

❖ **Discussion**

When working with older students, you can give them a questionnaire to determine their personal learning style or preference. The questionnaire can be a true/false format and may include items that resemble the following:

☐ I learn best when I am listening to the teacher.

☐ I learn best when the teacher writes on the board.

☐ I like when we write words in the air.

☐ I like to make pictures or diagrams.

☐ I like to study and say the facts out loud.

☐ I like when the teacher uses learning games.

☐ I have trouble taking notes as the teacher talks.

☐ I do not like to draw pictures or diagrams.

By determining the learning styles of your class, you can individualize instruction and make it more meaningful to your students. For example, if you learn that most of the students are visual learners, you can add more pictures to your lessons, use an overhead projector, do diagrams, and write notes on the board. You can also do more cooperative group work that involves making collages, posters, and charts.

Determining learning styles is an important aspect of getting to know your students. They will be more successful if you can adapt your methods to meet their needs. They will feel more comfortable if instruction is not geared toward one learning style.

As a fourth grade teacher, I found it overwhelming, at times, to adapt to the various learning styles and abilities of my students. It became clear that many students were not retaining information I taught the day before, let alone the month before. I was intrigued, however, when they each knew the words to every song they had ever heard.

I thought back to my own childhood and realized I knew the words to numerous songs that I knowingly tried to memorize. The connection between music and retention became clear. I decided to take our science unit and make songs out of the content.

*With no musical accompaniment, the students began to 'rap' the words to a song called, **Rotation and Revolution.** It seemed that each child, regardless of primary learning style, responded exceptionally well. I continued to write songs for the material we were studying and tested student retention throughout the year. Students not only retained the material throughout the year, they retained it to this day. When I have the pleasure of running into a former student, they still sing this song to me:*

"Ro-ta-tion, its spinning without breaks.
Ro-ta-tion, day and night is what it makes.
Ro-ta-tion, it's what we're learning.
Ro-ta-tion, means the Earth is turning."

Never underestimate the power of music and do not be dismayed if you are not a natural rhymer! There are songs for almost every subject area and topic. Check your local teaching supply store, catalog, or website. One of my favorites is the School House Rock series, available on audio or video. - LW

Chapter 9

Do As I Say...Period

From day one, classroom management is an issue that will need constant attention and refinement. Regardless of your proficiency in a given subject area, without successful classroom management, instruction will be ineffective. It begins as soon as the students arrive and lasts until they have departed. Creating a classroom environment that is conducive to learning is not easy.

Maintaining Order

It requires much more energy to maintain order than to let things run out of control. The most important thing you can impart to your students is that they must do as you say...period, no questions asked. This is an important concept. You make the decisions in your classroom and you are the boss. You must be able to control your students' behavior and maintain an orderly environment.

Does this mean showing up with a whip? Of course not, we are educators, not lion tamers. You may have heard the warning, "Never smile until Thanksgiving." Actually, you can smile, *even on the first day of school,* as long as you are prepared to stop any behaviors that are unacceptable. Students will test the boundaries, even on the first day of school. The key is to assess the situation and respond immediately.

Find Your Style

Finding your own style of discipline will depend upon many factors. You must remember that what works today, may not work tomorrow and what works with one student, may not work with another. The reason is simple, you are dealing with real, live, breathing people. You are not working on an assembly line. Each student comes from a different background, has a different personality, and different moods.

Location and Population

Classroom management will also be affected by the location of your school. As they say in real estate…location, location, location. The neighborhood, the student population, the size of the school, and the grade levels served will have a significant effect on discipline policies. An inner city school that serves students from Grades K-6 will operate differently than a suburban school that services Grades K-2. A school with a population of 100 students will operate differently than a school with more than 1,000 students. It is critical that you know and understand your district's discipline policies. This is one area where you will cross paths with parents under tense, occasionally confrontational circumstances. If you are following district policy to the letter, you will have the support of your administration.

Where To Begin?

The question for many new teachers is, how do I successfully establish discipline procedures? What if the students do not take me seriously? What if I lose control of the class? These are all valid questions and examples of situations you will not want to occur. So, in reality, the most compelling question is, how can you successfully manage your classroom? Here are some strategies:

School Policies

Before the school year begins, discuss discipline policies with your principal. Find out what is expected of the students and the consequences for inappropriate behavior. Keep in mind that discipline policies vary from school to school, even within the same district. You will need to determine when it is appropriate to contact parents, to request administrative assistance, and whether suspensions are given. Once you understand your administration's expectations, it will be easier for you to establish your own classroom policies.

Rules and Consequences

The first step in maintaining positive classroom management is having definite rules and consequences. This should be addressed on the first day of school and reinforced throughout the year. With young students, you may even want to incorporate student ideas to create class rules and consequences. For all students, use positive language when establishing class rules. Rather than *Do Not Call Out*, try using *Raise Your Hand To Speak*. This method clearly expresses the expectations you have for your class and leaves little room for doubt.

Once the rules are established, it would be wise to have your principal review them. This will ensure that they comply with district policies and provide a forum for feedback. If they are approved, that is wonderful. If changes are requested, be sure to comply. It is also imperative that each rule is clear and understandable.

> While your rules will be established before the school year begins, it is sometimes difficult to anticipate every problem you will need to address. If you encounter a situation that was not included in the rules, you can always add it in later. Just be sure to notify parents and students, as you would with your original classroom rules and consequences.

The following is a sample of classroom rules written in a positive tone. It is the subtle use of positive language, as opposed to negative language, that encourages students to comply. Rules should always be adjusted for grade level and environment, but most rules will be a variation of the following:

Class Rules

1. Walk at all times.

2. Raise your hand to speak.

3. Keep your hands and feet to yourself at all times.

4. Be kind to others.

5. Use an inside, quiet voice while working.

6. Play nicely during recess.

7. Work carefully and neatly.

8. Push in your chair when leaving your desk or table.

9. Keep your classroom clean.

10. Cooperate and share.

When you are confident that your students understand the rules, you must introduce them to the consequences. It is important to spend as much time explaining the consequences as you spend explaining the rules. The following is a sample list of possible consequences:

List of Consequences

• After the first offense, write the student's name on the board and remind them of the rule they have broken.

• After the second offense, place a check next to the student's name and speak to them in private.

• After the third offense, place a second check next to the student's name and take away a privilege.

• After the fourth offense, place a third check next to the student's name and contact a parent. Depending upon the severity of the offense, it may be necessary to contact the principal at this point.

When establishing consequences, use discretion and distinguish between the most serious rules and those not as serious.

Your style as a disciplinarian will greatly depend upon many factors. Think about your grade level, the size of your class, and your students. Positive reinforcement is a tool that encourages good behavior. To effectively implement this method, it should be geared to your students' level and interests. The following are examples of how to positively reinforce appropriate behavior:

Strategies For The Class

Fill The Jar

Keep a jar on your desk and drop a marble in each time the class accomplishes an objective. Always acknowledge good behavior, whether it is as simple as quietly clearing off their desks or as serious as a fire drill. Think of a prize for filling the jar and sporadically remind them of their goal. Deposit one marble for simple tasks, several for complicated ones.

Change Your Strategies

Be willing to identify the needs of your students and change your strategies accordingly. If the class has been struggling with a lesson and you can see the frustration mounting, switch gears. Try an impromptu spelling bee. Read a book or a chapter from a book that the class has been enjoying. Have everyone drop their pencils and take a walk. Whether you walk through the building or take it outside, it may diffuse their frustration and prevent problems from arising.

Never Tolerate Peer Harassment

Be clear that you will **not tolerate** students making fun of one another. Throughout the school year, the class becomes a second family and students should be encouraged to watch out for one another. Instruct them to report to you if a student in your class or in another classroom is harassing someone from the class. This is an area where you will want to be especially firm. A school should not be a place of terror or dread for any student and as a teacher, you have a responsibility to be aware of all aspects of their lives and to provide a safe environment.

Mediate All Conflicts

To avoid the escalation of small disputes, be sure students understand that you will mediate all conflicts. Students must realize that, regardless of who instigates a conflict, they must bring it to you. If not, all parties will bear the consequences. All too often a student is drawn into a situation and words escalate into shoving. At this point, both students are wrong. It may seem unfair and many parents will argue that their child was merely defending himself or herself, but the reality of the situation is more complex. While students are under your supervision, they are not to instigate or respond to disputes. It only takes seconds for a minor scuffle to become a dangerous situation. Be clear that **you will handle any and all situations that arise.**

Strategies For Individual Students

Invest In A Binder

As mentioned throughout the book, it is imperative that you maintain excellent records and notes. This should include student behavior. An easy way to collect this data is with a binder. Develop a form that will make it easy for you to input information in a timely manner. Make several copies of the form for each student. Arrange the forms alphabetically in the binder. Include information such as date, location, description of behavior, and actions taken. If you spoke to a student 3 times regarding staying seated, be sure that information is recorded. Also, be sure that your students understand that any and all behavior will be shared with their parents. Also, keep this binder in a locked drawer or cabinet, as it may be tempting for a student facing disciplinary action to destroy or hide the binder.

Weekly Review

Meet with students weekly to review their progress, both academic and behavioral, and discuss ideas for improvement. Be sure to praise positive behavior and achievements and build your students' trust.

Keep Families Informed

Keep in close contact with each student's family. This includes a quick phone call to let them know that their son or daughter had a great week and continues to excel, as well as information regarding inappropriate behavior or difficulties in a subject area.

Consistency Counts

Be consistent in both your enforcement of rules and the consequences. If three students break a rule and go unpunished, it is not fair to punish the fourth student for the same offense. This is also true for the consequences. Once a consequence is established, you must follow through with the same consequence for everyone, without exception.

The Punishment Must Fit The Crime

You must think carefully about your consequences. An effective consequence that is overused will lose its effectiveness. The best defense is a great offense. Remember, your goal is to have order in the classroom, not to spend half of your day sending children to the principal. Discipline takes time and you want to identify situations before they escalate and eliminate them before they devour instructional time.

> When dealing with an individual student, try to assess the cause of the behavior. Try to determine if the student is having difficulties at home or in school. Helping a student solve a problem will help you gain his or her trust while reducing disruptions. Remember, the causes are not always obvious.

Instruction As A Management Tool

Your instructional style will directly affect the number of disruptions you deal with on a daily basis. Here are some strategies for utilizing instruction as a way to reduce discipline issues:

Do Not Teach From Your Desk

CEO's and Bank Presidents work from their desks, teachers walk the room. You cannot see what your class is doing if you are anchored to your desk. Classroom management will also suffer if you stand in front of the room without moving. Moving around the room keeps students on their toes and involved. It also provides you with a bird's-eye view of who is on task and who is not. Often times, simply standing near a student who is about to act up will deter the behavior.

Your Voice Is The Window To Your Soul

Modulate your voice and your tone. Students should be able to tell, by the sound of your voice, if you are disturbed with their behavior. Your voice should not be meek or nervous, it should exude confidence. Do not scream at your class or raise your voice for every offense. When you need to raise your voice, it should mean something to the class. If you constantly raise your voice, the students will not notice and you will lose an effective method of classroom control.

Remember, it is not always necessary to increase the volume of your voice to gain control of your class. Simply change your tone and facial expression and a student will know you mean business. Effective methods include turning off the lights, ringing a bell, or using non-verbal cues.

Silence Is Golden

By the same token, silence can also be a powerful tool. If you notice a problem developing, stop speaking in the middle of a sentence and wait for the class to compose themselves.

Getting To Know You

The seats you assign will have a tremendous impact on the behavior of your students. It is a good idea to avoid group seating until you have had a week to get to know the personality types and learning styles of your students. You will soon learn which students have vision or hearing problems and need to be near the board. You will quickly learn which students tend to be disruptive or have little self-control. They should be separated from students with similar traits and be seated as close to you as possible.

Please Remain Seated

Students should remain in their seats at all times, unless they have requested *and received* permission to do otherwise. This is important, as students who are permitted to roam freely have a much greater chance of getting into trouble. All movement should be supervised.

Go With The Flow

Be flexible in your instruction and go with the flow. As the year progresses, you will notice patterns of behavior that are contingent upon external forces. A very hot classroom will not only contribute to poor performance, it will also lend itself to discipline issues. An effective teacher can identify issues that will obstruct progress and adjust instruction. This is a very important facet of teaching. You will need to learn that your lesson plan book is a guide and not set in stone. It is more productive to postpone a lesson and address the needs of your students, than to forge ahead with little regard to your effectiveness. Keep the following factors in mind:

Time Of Day Matters

When preparing lessons, be sensitive to your students' abilities and also the time of day. Adults tend to overlook that children are especially sensitive to the time of day. A hands-on science activity may be more successful in the morning, even if it means changing the schedule for the day. After lunch and recess, children, like adults, become tired. Creating a situation where tired children need to perform complex tasks may trigger extreme frustration. By the end of your first few weeks, as the students have settled into their new routine, you will be able to see patterns developing. If they have a late lunch, try not to schedule a complicated subject prior to the meal. On the same note, first thing in the morning is usually when students are at their optimal performance levels.

Too Hot To Trot

The same is true for temperature. It is very difficult to concentrate in extreme heat. If the temperature is out of your control and increasingly uncomfortable, be sensitive to how it will affect your students and adjust accordingly. In addition to temperature, be aware of weather. If a thunderstorm or blizzard occurs at the beginning of your lesson on prepositions, you may want to break stride and discuss weather. Rather than forbidding the students to gaze out of the window, encourage them to watch the storm and write about it.

You Can't Fight The Holidays

The excitement of an upcoming holiday or school event has the potential to cause enormous disruptions. If Halloween falls on a school day, do not expect to accomplish difficult tasks or introduce new material that day. You are working with children and your beautiful lesson on the Mid-Atlantic States will pale in comparison. This may be a great opportunity to play a trivia game pertaining to material you are teaching.

Applying Your Strategies

Once you are familiar with the school's discipline policies, have established your own classroom rules, and familiarized yourself with instructional strategies to limit disruptions, you are ready to apply this knowledge to your classroom. We have provided some important tips for maintaining classroom control.

No Two Students Are The Same

Each student is different and each day is different. Like adults, students have bad days, too. Try to assess the needs of each student and respond accordingly. Be sensitive to the student who never gets in trouble and suddenly finds himself/herself in trouble regularly. This may be an indication that something is wrong.

Less Is Best

Handle as many issues as you can on your own. Many new teachers make the mistake of requesting assistance for every minor infraction. Your management style will be judged by your administrators, colleagues, parents, and even your students. You do not want the reputation of being unable to control your students and in constant need of assistance. If you send for the principal when minor situations arise, this option will lose its effectiveness when you truly need it.

Know When To Ask For Help

Remember, the safety of each student is your responsibility and you must use common sense and district policies as your guide. Anything that could be dangerous to the students or to yourself, needs to be reported immediately. If a student has challenged your authority and the situation is escalating, it is wise to call for assistance. Do not wait until the situation is out of control.

Keep Your Hands To Yourself

There is no situation that permits you to raise your hands to a student. The days of corporal punishment are long gone and a slight tap could be career ending. If two students are fighting, do your best, verbally, to end the fight. If you must physically break it up, do so carefully or wait until there is another adult to assist. Too many teachers have been hospitalized as a result of breaking up fights. If you are pregnant, summon help immediately. Do not put yourself or your unborn child at risk.

Big Brother

Always behave as if your actions are being video taped and do not allow your temper to cloud your judgement. If you feel as though you are about to lose your temper, step back and take a deep breath, call for a neighboring teacher to assist, or turn out the lights and calm the environment down. Do not act out of anger or frustration. Students, like all children, will test you, push you to your limits, and purposely try to force a reaction from you. Remember, you are the adult and you will not be able to say, "He started it!"

Words *Can* Hurt

It is important to be aware of the language you use in the presence of your students. While everyone knows that obscenities are off limits, there are other words that should never be used. These include *shut up, I'll kill you, and leave me alone.* It is common knowledge that words can do more damage than a physical attack, and children are much more sensitive to what we say to them than we realize. It will be difficult, but always remember that you are the professional and they are the children, no matter how frustrated you feel!

Once Upon A Time

Use stories to keep student interest elevated and reduce disruptions. In the middle of a lesson, tell the class a personal story related to the topic. Nothing draws a daydreamer back on task like a story. If you do not have a personal story, use a current event.

> *As a person of Italian origin, I grew up using the expression 'Mama Mia' in my everyday vocabulary. I was never taught to speak Italian, but my students were so fascinated with the expression, that they asked me to teach them Italian.*
>
> *Not wanting to lose their enthusiasm, I began my Italian lessons. I told them that 'stracciatelle' meant put their heads down. I told them that 'manja' meant be quiet. I told them that 'bella faccia' meant to clear their desks. Of course, these three expressions mean egg drop soup, eat, and beautiful face.*
>
> *Throughout the day I would give numerous directions in English and Italian, although most of my Italian words were the names of food. The students loved it, although the Italian Police Officer that came in for the D.A.R.E. program always looked confused when he entered the room. He could never quite figure out why, every time I said egg drop soup in Italian, my students put their heads down.*
>
> *By the last week of school, I felt it was time to confess that I didn't understand a word of Italian and we did a fun lesson on what the expressions really meant. They were shocked to see a box of pastina and realize it didn't mean sit down!*
>
> *The following year, when my former students would walk by my room and hear me teaching Italian to my new students, they would give me a big wink. - LW*

So Long Apples and Oranges

Use topics that interest your students when teaching. Simply stated, when giving the children a word problem, instead of apples and oranges, use elephants and kangaroos, video games, music and movie stars, sports teams, etc. Their attention will be elevated and you will see a difference in participation.

A Day In The Life Of...

Find out what your students do on the weekends and if possible, show up. If several students play for the local little league, find out what time and catch a couple of games, even if you can only stay for 20 minutes. While the games will not be exciting, your presence will be thrilling to the students and their parents.

Draw The Line

Do not try to befriend your students. Many new teachers make the mistake of thinking the students will respond better if they are their friends. Unfortunately, for these teachers, this is never the case. Children will need to respect you as the adult, as the authority figure, as the teacher. This does not mean that the students dislike you. Your students just need to know where the line is and you have to be sure that line is clear.

> Many student teachers and first year teachers dread the discipline aspect of teaching. Some are under the misguided impression that the best way to get students to comply with classroom policies is to befriend them. This seem like a plausible idea; however, this becomes another slippery slope. There must be a level of respect between teacher and student for discipline to be effective. Trying to befriend your students will backfire and make the task of regaining control a tricky proposition.

The Keys To The Kingdom

When it comes to successful classroom management, the key is to establish effective policies from the moment the students enter your room and consistently follow through on those policies:

❖ Utilize non-verbal strategies.

❖ Make eye contact.

❖ Accentuate the positive.

❖ Recognize admirable behavior.

❖ *Never forget to breathe!*

There will be days when you feel as though you cannot stand another moment or that your head will spontaneously combust. These are the times when you must count to 10, remain calm, and breathe. Your actions and responses to student behavior will diffuse or ignite a situation. Preventing potential problems and immediately addressing inappropriate behavior will enable you to maintain order while providing effective instruction.

Remember, you were once a student who wanted to have fun in school. If your students respect you as an authority figure, you will be able to share a laugh or a joke with the class, without risking mayhem. You are the teacher and your students should do as you say...***period!***

Chapter 10

How Do I Assess Thee? Let Me Count The Ways

There are many methods teachers use to assess the students in their class. Each day, you will assess the knowledge your students have gained to gauge progress and construct lessons for the following day. Assessment is the driving force of teaching. While this may sound harsh, it is actually meant to be a positive thought. This does not mean 'teaching to the test'. Conversely, you need to adjust your instruction to meet the needs of all your students and to enable them to be successful.

For example, if you are working on teaching your second graders how to tell time and most of them are struggling, you'll need to come up with other strategies to reinforce the concept. The test on telling time, therefore, should wait until you feel that most of your students have grasped the idea. An effective teacher is one who is able to evaluate daily successes and failures and plan the next day accordingly.

It is also important to realize that children, like adults, do not perform their best every single day. Whether it is because their dance recital went later than expected or because they were up most of the night worrying about a sick parent, children have difficult nights and days when they are not themselves. It is unrealistic to expect otherwise; therefore, it is good to look at assessment as an on-going process, rather than a record of tests given on specific days.

Assessing your students in an on-going manner, using a variety of assessment tools, gives them numerous opportunities to succeed. Children have different learning styles and assessment should complement those styles. For example, some students may be more visual than others. For this type of student, an oral test can be extremely difficult. They would benefit more by drawing a picture or working on a project to show their understanding. In addition, not all students are good test takers. Unfortunately, most children do not know how to take a test properly. As part of your instruction, you should frequently model proper test taking strategies.

It is vital that you become aware of your school's assessment policy. The following list includes methods that may be used with most grade levels and types of learners.

Portfolio Assessment

Many schools are currently using a form of portfolio assessment. Portfolios consist of individual folders that contain daily work samples and specific tasks completed by the students. Assessment is conducted often and many times the students are not even aware that they are being "tested." Anecdotal records and observations are made by the teacher and are also included in each student's portfolio.

Portfolio assessment includes a series of checklists to be completed by the teacher near the end of the school year. The checklists use a rating scale, as opposed to a grading system. They are based upon benchmarks devised for each grade level. The benchmarks are closely related to the curriculum for that grade level. Portfolios are more subjective than traditional report cards and are much more informative. Parents are provided with a complete picture of how their child has grown since the beginning of the school year. The portfolios travel with the child to each grade level. The file grows each year and is eventually sent home when the child graduates from the school.

Standardized Tests

Many schools use some type of standardized test to assess the growth of the students. These tests are often used to determine if a student is in need of some form of basic skills instruction. These tests are usually administered in the spring and regular classroom instruction is postponed during this time. Although they can be beneficial to class placement and recognizing student needs, test scores are often misread and confusing to most parents. For the students, this type of testing can be overwhelming and scary. Try to alleviate their fears prior to testing.

When administering any kind of standardized test, it is important to try to keep the students as relaxed as possible. Keep your classroom quiet and remind students to eat a good breakfast. Separate the desks as best you can and play some fun, relaxing games when you are not testing. It may also be a good idea to refrain from giving any homework during this week.

Unit Tests, Chapter Tests, and Quizzes

These types of assessment are probably the most common and easiest to administer. They are often found in teaching manuals or within units of study in Science or Social Studies. They usually follow a similar format and assess students on what they have just learned. Here are a few hints when using these types of models:

Before The Test:

- ❖ Ensure ample time for review and studying.

- ❖ Provide a study guide for the children to complete.

- ❖ Implement cooperative review work to reach children with different learning styles.

- ❖ Play a game that highlights major topics covered.

- ❖ Make flashcards of the information.

During The Test:

❖ Have children stand a folder up for privacy from their neighbors.

❖ Read the directions together to be sure that every one understands what they are expected to do.

❖ If feasible, have the children highlight the directions so that they remember to complete all parts.

❖ Encourage students to check their work.

❖ Have them give you a signal on each page so that you know they have checked their work. For example, you may ask your class to draw a happy face on the top right hand corner of each page of their test when they have checked it over. Do not accept a test unless you see the happy faces on the corner of every page. This strategy helps the students remember to look at every sheet of the test *and to check their work.*

❖ Make sure that each student has something to do when they are finished with their test. They should have a book to read or a fun sheet to work on (Crossword puzzle, word search, coloring sheet). It can make some students very anxious to see that other children are finished with their test while they are still trying to complete it.

❖ Do not allow students to get out of their seats and hand in their test. Collect the tests when you observe that they are finished.

❖ Walk around the classroom during the test to answer questions and to check on progress.

❖ Keep the classroom as quiet as possible.

❖ Limit interruptions.

❖ Have each student sharpen their pencils before the test begins.

For extra credit, you may have them complete the following sentences on the back of the test:

◆ I learned…

◆ I enjoyed…

◆ I want to learn…

These simple sentences may provide valuable information and help you plan your next unit or chapter. You can also ask them to explain something they learned during the unit, but were not tested on.

After The Test:

❖ Return corrected tests to the students as soon as possible. It is important to review the test and the correct answers while the material is still fresh in their minds.

❖ If necessary, offer the opportunity to re-test.

❖ Have parents sign and return the tests.

❖ Keep excellent records of scores/grades.

❖ Be discreet. It is not necessary to share a student's results with the class.

❖ Write encouraging words of praise on every test regardless of the grade, like *Good Try* or *Great Idea.*

❖ Use the test scores to evaluate your teaching.

❖ If you do not feel that a particular test was a fair indication of what the students have learned, create a different test or assessment method.

For many students, the moment they complete a difficult test, they are filled with relief and forget that other students are still testing. They may try to speak to other students, pull materials out of their desk, or even sing to themselves. It is extremely important to keep the classroom as quiet and calm as possible.

Whether it is a standardized test or a quick math quiz, there will be significant differences in the time students will require. Instruct students, prior to testing, on what you expect from them as they finish. You may want to have materials available, such as word puzzles or comic books, that you can trade them for their tests. This will eliminate students digging through their desks and creating a disruption.

Avoid pressuring students that take longer to complete a quiz or test. While it is appropriate to remind students to keep an eye on the time or alert them when they have 10 minutes remaining, you do not want to harass them. If they feel that others are finished and you have become impatient, they are likely to start guessing or turn in an incomplete test. There is a certain level of stress associated with testing and you do not want to add to it.

Assessment Throughout The Year

The following are other types of assessment that should be incorporated into your school year:

Writing Samples

Various samples can be kept to show growth in writing. Be sure to keep samples of all stages of writing – brainstorming, rough draft, editing techniques, and final copy.

Informal Reading Inventories / Miscue Analysis

This is a procedure used to determine a student's instructional reading level. A student reads a passage aloud, while the teacher records how he/she reads each word in the text. It is used to analyze student miscues when reading orally. It helps determine the type of reader and the strategies used during reading.

Retellings or Story Mapping

This is a procedure by which a student retells a story and includes the major events and story elements. It can be written down or completed orally with a picture.

Spelling Inventories

This is a list of words that the students are asked to spell without studying. Each word on the list represents a different spelling pattern or phonetic rule.

Audiotapes

By recording the students reading orally, 2 – 3 times during the school year, you will be able to measure the growth in their oral reading skills.

Anecdotal Records/Teacher Observations

These are notes written by the teacher and kept in a confidential folder used to support grades given on a report card. This type of assessment measures participation, cooperation, and social skills.

Cloze Passages

This is procedure that is used to test comprehension by using context clues and determining missing vocabulary words.

To summarize, you should never use only one or two methods of assessment, but a combination of many. Through continual assessment, you should able to utilize various methods to gauge student progress, as well as your own teaching strengths.

Chapter 11

<u>Come One, Come All</u>

There are many special events throughout the school year that enable a new teacher to shine. These events are extremely important to the children in your class and they will remember them for the rest of their lives. Think back for a moment...do you remember your school play? Did you ever participate in a class bake sale? Were you ever chosen to make a speech or read your poetry in front of an audience? You can probably still remember the costume you wore in the play.

Now, it is your turn to create such lasting memories and experiences for your students and their families. Throughout the year there will be events, scheduled by the school, in which you will be required to participate. There will also be opportunities for you to develop your own events with your class. The following is a chronological list of some of the special events you may encounter during your first year:

Back To School Night

The first special event of the year may be Back-To-School night. This is an evening event when parents are invited to visit the school to learn about you, your classroom, your expectations and rules, and an overview of objectives for the school year. It usually takes place in September or early October and is an important meeting. Here are some helpful hints on how to make your first Back-To-School Night a success:

Preparing A Speech

If delivering a speech is part of the agenda, prepare your speech and know it well. It is important to talk to your principal to find out what exactly is expected of you at Back-To-School night. By speaking with other teachers in your school, you can learn how the evening should flow and what to expect. It is a good idea to write down the major topics you wish to discuss. Using index cards may work best, as you can flip to the next card easily. It is important to speak slowly and to make eye contact with each and every parent while you are speaking.

Preparing Your Classroom

Prepare your classroom by having the students' work clearly displayed. Clean up any clutter that may be in the way. Have the students write a short note or letter welcoming their parents to their classroom. They will enjoy reading them and writing back after the night is over. In the event that a parent cannot attend, you should write a note to the student telling him or her how proud you are of their work. Also, allow the student to bring home the note, hand-outs from the evening and samples of their work to share with their parents.

A Picture *Is* Worth A Thousand Words

For a quick and easy bulletin board idea, take pictures of each child in your class during the first week of school. You can display them and have children write about what they are doing in the picture. Children grow so much during a school year and a picture really captures that growth.

Dress For Success

Dress professionally. Your attire will show that you are a professional and establish a high level of respect. When in doubt about an outfit, **do not wear it**.

Breaking The Ice

If you will be speaking to the group, begin with a cheerful hello and a smile. Introduce yourself and ask for the audience's attention. Welcome the parents to your classroom and thank them for coming. Briefly discuss your handout.

All In A Day's Work

Discuss a typical day in your class. Parents are interested in knowing what goes on in school, since the standard answer they receive from their child is, *"Nothing."* Take them through a regular day, perhaps using slides or a video. This is an effective way to gain their attention and trust and it also demonstrates that you care about their children. The parents can "see" their children smiling and working during a typical day and the response is wonderful. If you are really feeling creative, you may even play some background music.

The Fine Print

Explain your classroom rules and your homework policy so that parents understand them. You should include them in your handout so that parents have the procedure in writing. Of course, this type of document should be approved by your principal.

Time For The Wish List

Request any special materials, such as egg cartons, paper towel rolls, and plastic bottles that you may need for projects. Again, you should include a list in your handout so that parents can refer to it.

Please Sign On The Dotted Line

Ask for volunteers for various classroom activities and parties. Hang sign-up sheets on the door and at the end of your speech, explain the purpose of the sheets. Ask parents to volunteer, if they are able.

Have A Nice Day

Thank the parents for coming and reassure them that you are ready to help them in any way necessary to ensure that their children have a wonderful year. Encourage them to come to you with questions or concerns and to keep the lines of communication open.

No Sidebars Please

If they have questions or concerns, request that they contact you to set up a conference (by phone or in-person). Remind them that this evening is **NOT for individual conferences**, but to enjoy the classroom and their child's work.

Be Careful What You Ask For

DO NOT ask your audience if there are any questions. Simply tell the group that you would be happy to answer questions individually when you have finished speaking to the group. The following story illustrates the danger of opening the floor to *any* question. As a new teacher, you do not want to be stumped by an unanticipated question in front of the group. If you are asked a question and do not know the answer, do not lie. Assure the parents that you will get back to them with a definite answer as soon as possible.

> *I had the misfortune of asking for questions during a Back-To-School Night speech and I was put in a very uncomfortable situation. I was asked a very difficult, if not impossible, question in front of the parents whose trust I had just gained. As my cheeks grew red, I wished I could take that moment back. Since the question was rather specific, I provided the parent with a general answer and later we spoke privately. - LB*

Put It In Writing

Provide parents with a handout so that they can remember the key points mentioned during the evening. In the handout, include a short list of broad major objectives for the school year. You should also mention any do's and don'ts. For example, you may ask parents for a week's notice when sending in a birthday treat, providing you with ample time to check the calendar and to prepare. You may also wish to explain the procedure for missed classwork.

The Ten Cent Tour

Allow parents some time to look at the things in the classroom and to write back to their child. There may also be a class parent that may request some time to speak or to collect money. Introduce this parent to the group.

Work The Room

Mingle with the group and say hello to as many parents as you can. Try not to allow one parent to take up all of your time.

Halloween

In the month of October, Halloween will be the focus of attention. Instead of trying to force the students into working on regular class work during such an exciting time, try to incorporate Halloween themes into your lessons.

Incorporate Theme Into Instruction

Allow the children to write scary stories as a creative writing assignment or write word problems about ghosts and witches during math.

Learn The Routine

Familiarize yourself with the school's Halloween policy. Talk with other teachers on your grade level or with your principal. You will need to know the following:

❖ Do the students dress in costumes?

❖ Is it for the entire day or just after lunch?

❖ Do the teachers dress up?

❖ Is there a theme for the teachers' costumes?

❖ Will each class have a party?

❖ Which class parents will help at the party?

❖ What types of games will be played?

❖ What type of treats will be served?

❖ Will there be a school parade?

Make sure that you are prepared for the day. Have extra Halloween books available in case the class gets too excited. You can always gather them for a story to regain control without spoiling the festive mood. It is also wise to have an extra costume handy for a child who may not have one.

> Many holiday celebrations involve treats and goodies that are filled with sugar. If you will be having a party, you may want to provide healthier treats, such as fruit kabobs or frozen juice bars. There are many delicious alternatives to candy that will not rev up a room full of children. If the children do have candy, try to limit the amount they may eat in school or have them take treats home to eat.

Parent Teacher Conferences

Usually your first parent-teacher conferences will be held in the fall. The conferences are generally scheduled in conjunction with the first report card. Here are some tips for successful conferences:

Prove Your Point

Be sure you have documentation to support the grades given to a student or the comments you have made.

At Your Fingertips

Write notes on index cards to remember everything you wanted to talk about with the parent.

That's All The Time We Have Folks

Stick to the allotted time. If it seems like a parent is going over the scheduled time, kindly ask the parent if you could continue the conference at a later date.

Just So We're On The Same Page

Set a goal for each student and share that goal with the parent. Discuss each student academically, behaviorally and socially.

A Second Date

If there is cause for concern, set up another time to discuss the student's growth before the next report card period or conference.

Speaking Of Great Kids

Always begin the conference with a positive statement about the student.

Thanksgiving and December Holidays

With Thanksgiving and the December holidays right around the corner, you must think about how to handle the different backgrounds and beliefs of your class. The best thing you can do for all holidays is to check with other teachers on your grade level and consult with your principal, if necessary. When it comes to holiday celebrations and class parties, you want to be in line with other teachers on your grade level. It would not be fair to the other students in the grade level if you decided to have a Thanksgiving party and the other classes did not. When having class parties here are a few tips to make them even more enjoyable:

Pow Wow With The Parents

Prior to the party, discuss the plans with the parents who will be in charge. Allow parents to be as involved as you feel comfortable. If you do not have parents to assist, plan a reasonable party that you will be able to arrange by yourself, with another class, or your grade level.

The Menu

Discuss the snacks that will be provided and be aware of any food allergies. Try to lean toward healthy snacks and consider snacks that do not require silverware or make a mess.

Your Safety Net

Be prepared. Stock up on some fun stories or videos in case the party becomes too rowdy. You can always calm the class down by gathering them for a story or video.

Time Is Not On Your Side

No matter how much time you allot, it will not seem like enough . You will also want to enjoy the party you have planned. Prepare as much as you can ahead of time and have student volunteers help with the set up.

If you find that you have more time than you need, you can always fill the time with a story if necessary.

Manners Matter

Make sure that your class uses manners. Remind your students, before the party, of the behavior that is expected of them. During the party, comment when you hear a child using appropriate manners. At the end of the party, remember to thank all of the helpers.

An Advanced Screening

Review any books or videos that the students wish to share with the class. You should be aware of the rating *and the contents* of any videos and the appropriateness of any books with which you may be unfamiliar.

The Cleaning Crew

Expect the students to clean up. Do not expect parent helpers to be the cleaning service. Also, do not leave your room a mess for the custodian or cleaning staff. Allow 10 minutes for the children to pitch in and help clean your room.

Rules Still Apply

Remember that, regardless of the event, you are still the teacher and need to discipline any students that do not follow the rules or act inappropriately. It is very easy for a party to run out of control if you do not maintain order.

With so many different holidays to celebrate in December, you may opt for a winter party that does not focus on one particular celebration or a variety of small parties highlighting each occasion. However you decide to handle the December holidays, be sure to check with your principal and involve students and parents as much as possible.

Talent Shows

At some point during the school year, your school may hold a Talent Show or a School Play. If there is a talent show, find out if all classes participate. If they do, get involved. You will want to show your support and encourage your students to take part. Here are some tips:

The Show Must Go On

If the school does not have a talent show or a school play, you may wish to have your own with your class. It does not need to be elaborate, it should simply be enjoyable to the students.

Consultations

Check with your principal and then ask the teachers on your grade level to see if they would like to join you. This is an activity that you will want to share with as many students as possible.

Spread The Word

Send out notices and get permission slips, if necessary. Invite parents to help with organization or set-up.

One For All...

Have your students help with as much of the organization as possible. Invite parents and ask for volunteers with costumes, music, and scenery.

Review The Rules

Remind students about their behavior and about what you expect of them during rehearsals and the actual show. Events of this nature can become very stressful and the last thing you will want to worry about is a disruptive class.

This type of event allows all students to shine. It is important to offer such opportunities to your students, as everyone in your class will be able to participate and grow through the experience. Remember that it does not have to be an elaborate production, but an experience that the students will never forget.

Assemblies

Your class will be invited to many assemblies during the course of the school year. Before you attend your first assembly, it is important to review the class rules and discuss appropriate behavior. The assembly may be an author, a choir, or an organization that visits schools to entertain or discuss an important topic. Keep the following points in mind:

Sit And Stay Awhile

It is a good idea for you to sit with your class and pay attention to the performance. The students will pick up on your interest and will act up if you are not engaged in the assembly.

Coverage Considerations

If your special is during the assembly time, check with the special area teacher to see if they will be coming to relieve you or if they wish to reschedule your class.

Do Not Leave Children Unattended

Do not leave your class unattended. Even though there are many teachers in the room, your class is your responsibility.

Thank You, Thank You Very Much

After the assembly, be sure to have your class send a thank you note. You can make a class note or have the students make individual notes. The Parent Teacher Organization often sponsors these events, and they appreciate hearing if the students enjoyed them.

Bake Sales

Another memorable event is a Bake Sale. Whether it is to purchase a tree for the front of the school or to adopt-a-whale, teachers generally have bake sales to raise money for a specific cause. In addition, a bake sale is a wonderful way to teach your students about money. Here are some helpful tips:

Baking Permit

It is pertinent that you get approval from your principal to host a bake sale.

Making Dough With Dough

You will then need to involve parents, since the success of your bake sale will depend upon their support. Work closely with parents to organize what to sell, who will provide items, and how much to charge.

It Pays To Advertise

Get organized and have the children help make posters and notices. Spread the word throughout the school and distribute notices to all students.

Take A Number

Set up time slots for classes to visit your bake sale to avoid a large crowd.

Spread The Word

After the sale, make an announcement and tell the student body how much money was raised.

Thank You, One and All

Send out thank you notes to the classes that attended.

Literary Tea

If you would like to have parents involved in a class project, you may want to host a Literary Tea. Parents are invited to come to the classroom to hear their children reading poetry or stories that they have written. In addition, the students will serve iced tea and a snack to the parents. It is a win-win situation. The class is excited because they get to share their writings and the parents are thrilled to be watching and listening to their children read their work. It requires very little preparation since they will simply be reading their writing. The following are suggestions for a wonderful Literary Tea:

You Are Cordially Invited

You will need to schedule about an hour for a class of 25 students and invite their parents to attend.

Tea And Crumpets

Decide what refreshments will be served, keeping in mind the age level of your students. Select items that require little preparation and will not leave crumbs all over your room.

A Little Time To Brag

Allow some time for questions and for the children to show off their classroom. This will be a new experience for many students and they will be very proud of their work.

Show Your Appreciation

Thank everyone involved in making the Literary Tea a memorable event. If pictures were taken, scan them into a computer and onto your thank you cards. Parents will be thrilled to see their child and have a memento of this special day.

Open House

Another special event that your school may hold is an Open House. This is a designated evening, usually in the spring when parents and students visit the classroom and celebrate their work. Unlike Back-To-School Night, the focus of Open House is on the students and their work from the school year; therefore, you will not need a prepared speech. Of course, you should be sure to find out exactly what is expected of you. If your school does have an Open House, these tips may help:

Spring Cleaning

Your classroom should be decorated appropriately and feel cheerful and welcoming. You should be sure that the room is neat and orderly and reflects your leadership.

Decisions, Decisions

The students may help you decide what work they wish to exhibit on their desks. Not every student will be proud of the same work. If there is a particular assignment that a student is proud of, allow them to display it for their parents.

Classroom As A Gallery

Hang students' work on a bulletin board, clothesline, or window. Every student in your class must be represented on all displays. Check to make sure that the spelling and grammar are correct on all written pieces.

Say Cheese

Remember those photographs you took of each student during the first week of school and displayed on Back-To-School Night? Save them and take a second photo of the children before Open House. Set up both photos on a simple bulletin board titled "See How We've Grown." Parents **love** to see pictures of their children.

Open House is also the perfect evening to thank parent volunteers that helped you during the school year. It is important, however, to remind parents that this evening is NOT an appropriate time to discuss their child's placement for the following year. In addition, you may suggest that families visit the classrooms of possible teachers for the upcoming school year. All in all, Open House is a pleasant evening – enjoy it!

Field Day

Near the end of the school year, you may have a Field Day. This is when the students participate in a variety of activities, usually outside. The activities may include a three-legged race, an egg race, potato sack races, and a water balloon toss. This type of event enables all students to do extremely well, regardless of academic ability. Here are some great ideas to ensure a successful day:

The Olympics Had To Start Somewhere

If your school does not offer a field day, you may wish to have your own. You may also want to have a class picnic on the same day.

Do I Have Any Volunteers?

Enlist some volunteers to help you set up the day and the picnic. Have a rain date in mind or a place to go if it rains.

Everyone Wins

Choose games that students of all athletic abilities can enjoy. Try to keep excessive competitiveness out of the event. Rather than having prizes for the winners, insist that it is a day of fun for everyone.

Enjoy!

Do not let the day slip away without being able to enjoy it. Reap the rewards of your hard work and have fun with your students.

On Your Mark, Get Set, Teach!

Special events that go beyond the curriculum are very important because they help you to reach every child. Your students will excel in these areas and feel good about themselves. It is important to offer such opportunities to your students in order to make their year a memorable and exciting one.

Chapter 12

On The Road Again

During the course of the school year, you will no doubt travel with your class. Whether it is a walking trip to the neighborhood firehouse or an overnight trip to another state, you must ensure that the students understand and accept your expectations. The same rules should apply, whether the students are in their classroom or an amusement park.

Depending upon the size of your school, you may not need to plan a class trip. In large schools where there are several classes for each grade level, trips will probably be planned by veteran teachers and include all classes. There may also be trips that your district has planned for your grade level, district-wide. In a small school or a school where each class does its own thing, you may need to plan a trip yourself or with another new teacher.

The success of a field trip begins with planning. There is no substitute for extensive planning. Here are some ideas for a successful trip:

Destination

When investigating a destination, there are several factors you must take into consideration. Is the destination age-appropriate? This is important to keep the students interested throughout the trip. A zoo is a wonderful, educational location for children in primary grades and will easily provide enough activity to keep your students busy. Once children reach the upper elementary grades, the zoo may be less interesting for several reasons. First and foremost, by ten years old, they may have visited the zoo several times with their families and with the school. Unless you are studying a specific unit related to animals, they may have little interest in a zoo. If your school is located near a science center, check to make sure that this venue is appropriate for youngsters. If the exhibits require reading and higher level concepts, young students may be bored.

On the other hand, older students may find this type of trip extremely interesting. The same holds true for museums. Before you commit to a trip, discuss the activities available for *your* students. If it is feasible, visit the destination on your own. You will know the attention span and interests of your students and should easily be able to determine if it is age appropriate.

Distance

Another important factor is distance. If you are lucky enough to have interesting destinations close to your school, distance will not be an issue. If however, you would like to visit a national monument that is 3 hours away, this will probably not be an option and a trip of this magnitude is not a wise choice for a first year teacher to plan. Distance must also be assessed in comparison to your grade level. While older children can handle a long bus ride, younger children may be so tired and cranky by the time they arrive that they will not be able to thoroughly enjoy the trip you have planned.

Transportation

When considering distance, you must also consider transportation. If you will be requesting a district school bus, the bus will not be available until all students have arrived at the school and must be back in time to bring students home. If you are using a private bus, you will need to check and see what time the bus is available and when you will need to return. You must also check to see how many students and chaperones the bus will hold. If the bus holds 55 people, but you have 60, you will need two buses.

Budget

In addition, budget will be a significant factor determining where you will be able to go. If the school has allotted a specific budget for trips, you must be sure that you do not go over budget. There are exceptions to this rule, however. If the PTA can contribute to the trip or the district will allow students to contribute to the expenses, budget will be less of an issue. If students are expected to pay, be sure that this will not create a hardship for student families. You do not want to plan a great trip and have three students left behind because they cannot afford the fee. In a suburban school, this may not be as much of an issue as in an urban, low income area. Be sensitive to the situations of all of your students.

Educational Value

Does your trip have educational value? Years ago class trips were seen as recreational activities. Things have changed a great deal since then. Now, before a trip is approved, you may need to explain the educational value in detail. Does it relate to material you are teaching in your class? If you are teaching a third grade unit on the solar system and you plan a trip to a local planetarium, your trip should be approved. If you suggest a trip to the batting cages, however, there is a good chance that your trip will be denied. Field trips are less about recreation and more about supplementing curriculum, and a trip that supports what you are teaching is likely to be approved and well received by your students.

Prepare Your Students

Once you have selected a destination, begin to prepare your students. Find a brochure and discuss the activities that your destination has to offer. Promote enthusiasm for the trip and then discuss the student's responsibilities for attending. Prior to the trip, student behavior should be evaluated and proper behavior should be a prerequisite for attending. Remind students that traveling with a class is an enormous responsibility and that you cannot bring students that may cause a problem. The privilege of attending the trip is for those who can conduct themselves as they would in school. If you have doubts about bringing a particular student, discuss your concerns with your principal.

Notify The Parents

Once you have shared the news with your class, you should send a letter home, notifying parents of the plans. Parents should also be aware of the behavior requirements for such trips and the possibility that their child may be excluded if he or she does not demonstrate appropriate behavior. As the trip date approaches, if you have students in jeopardy of not attending, parents should be aware of this possibility. It may damage your relationship with the parent if you wait until the day before the trip to notify them that their son or daughter will not be able to attend.

Chaperones

In addition to informing parents about the trip, you should invite parents to chaperone the trip. Each school has a different policy on the number of chaperones that you may take. If the number is low and inter-est is high, accept parents on a first come, first served basis. Invite other parents to meet the class at the destination and tag along with the group. If you can take along as many parents as you would like, take them all. Smaller groups are conducive to a successful trip and additional adult supervision should be welcome. On another note, it is wonderful when children can share a special day with a family member and know that they are more important than work.

Details

Once you have the trip set and the chaperones selected, you will need to work on the details. This includes lunch. You need to determine if the trip will be long enough to warrant lunch plans. Some trips are short and the students will return in time for lunch. Other trips, that will run through lunch time, will require much more planning. Some districts will send box lunches to the school on the morning of your trip. Several days before the trip, you will need to notify the cafeteria staff about your trip. They need to know that your class will not be in the cafeteria on that day, and they will also need to know how many lunches to provide. If this is not an option, you will need to find out if your destination has lunch available. Do they have a cafeteria or restaurant or just a picnic area? In this case, students will need to bring money or a lunch. If the parents have enough warning, either option should be fine.

Permission Slips

Two weeks before the trip, you should send out permission slips. Keep a list with the slips that are returned and check off the students that have returned their slip. Continue to remind students who have forgotten their slips. As the day of the trip approaches, call parents who have yet to return permission slips and explain the students will not be permitted to attend if a signed slip is not returned. This is one rule where you should never make an exception.

Making The Most Of Your Destination

As the trip nears, find out exactly what is offered at your destination. If there are shows that children will attend, find out what time and if your students will need a reservation. Popular destinations adhere to rigid schedules, and if you have not reserved seats for your students, they will not be admitted. If there are several shows, select those that are appropriate and make a schedule for chaperones and students to follow. When creating the schedule, leave plenty of time for walking around, visiting the gift shop and numerous requests for the bathroom. The following is an example of a schedule:

Good Morning Everyone,

Today is the day we have been eagerly awaiting, our class trip! We want to ensure that everyone has a wonderful time and will provide each person with important trip information.

Schedule

9:15 – Load buses. Mrs. A's Class will be on Bus 2.

9:30 – Depart for Scienceland.

10:15 – Arrive and register at Scienceland.

10:30 – Groups may tour independently, brochures will be distributed upon arrival.

11:15 – Solar Show – Planetarium A – 3rd Floor. Our group will meet by the fountain. Do not be late, doors lock at 11:25.

12:15 – Lunch in Picnic Area 2, located outside Planetarium A.

1:00 – Groups may tour independently and visit the Gift Shops. There is a different shop located on each floor.

2:00 – Board buses at the main entrance. Buses will need to depart at 2:10 sharp. **Do not be late.** Our bus is Yellow Bus # 245.

3:00 – Arrive at school.

If anyone has an emergency, I will have my cell phone with me or I can be paged in the building. My cell phone number is xxx-xxxx and the school number is xxx-xxxx. We will discuss the trip on the bus if anyone has any questions. Thank you for your cooperation, let's have a safe, fun day.

Mrs. A

Day Of The Trip Details

On the day of the trip, expect students and parents to be very excited and arrive very early. Have your essential paperwork in hand, including your class list and emergency phone numbers. Verify that you have all permission slips and turn copies of them into the school secretary before you depart. Keep track of all students as they arrive. If the departure time is nearing and a student has not arrived, call the house to see if you should expect him or her. As the chaperones arrive, introduce them to one another. Be sure that each one has a copy of the schedule and the names of the children in their group.

Safety Measures

If your students are young, give them each a name tag necklace with their name, their school, and your name. Tell them where they should go if they become separated from their group. Make them repeat it several times. Request that the chaperones show them the meeting place when they arrive. Also, insist that students find a security guard or adult who works at the establishment in the event they get lost. Once security is notified, many places will initiate a lock down.

Another factor that must be considered when traveling with your students is their safety. You must prepare them, even for the most simple of trips. Keep in mind that you are responsible for every student, whether they are in your group or with a parent chaperone. For this reason, safety should be stressed in the most serious manner. The following tips will help ensure a safe trip.

For Walking Trips:

❖ Prior to your outing, you should review the rules of the road. Your students should walk in a straight orderly line and know that they are never allowed near the street.

❖ While walking in line, they should be quiet and respectful of the people who live in the neighborhood. Excessive noise leads to chaos and this could pose many dangers. A silent line is easiest to control.

❖ Students should keep a brisk pace and a tight line, without large gaps. You should walk on the outside of the line, toward the middle. If you walk toward the front of the line, you will not have effective control of the back of the line. Have a trustworthy student, who will heed your commands, at the front of the line. Prepare the lead student to stop the line at all business driveways, alleyways and intersections. Instruct all students to remain in their place and never to pass the lead student.

❖ Keep a cell phone with you and provide the office with the path you will take. In the case of an emergency, this will ensure that you receive immediate assistance.

❖ Instruct students not to speak to strangers. If they are walking through their own neighborhood, it's okay for them to wave or say hello to people they know, but strangers should be off limits.

❖ When the class reaches an intersection, the lead student should hold the line and you should proceed to the corner. Check the intersection and make sure there are no cars in sight. If you are at a traffic light, do not cross until you have a new green light and be aware of cars that may be turning. As you enter the intersection, keep your hands extended, stand in the middle of the crosswalk and be sure that all cars in the vicinity see your students. Instruct children to walk briskly when in an intersection, but never run. Once all students are successfully across the street, return to your position in the middle of the line.

For Bus Trips:

❖ Bus behavior should be discussed before any and all bus trips. The bus driver should be able to drive in relative silence, and it will be up to you to establish the rules.

❖ As students board the bus, it is a good idea to seat the students in assigned seats. Keep all students that pose a potential problem near the front of the bus, under your watchful eye. Your students may be very disappointed with this arrangement and view trips as a time to let their hair down, but your objective on the bus is safety, not socialization.

❖ It is a good idea to instruct students to be silent on the bus ride. Yes, silent! This will keep the students calm for their arrival, eliminate distractions for the bus driver, and contribute to their safety. Again, many students and even some parents may not be happy with this idea, but this should be a strictly enforced rule. Don't worry, the bus driver will love you!

❖ Be sure students understand that if they do not cooperate or pose a safety problem, their parents will be called from the destination and asked to pick them up. This rarely ever needs to happen, but they should know that you will place their safety and the safety of their classmates over the inconvenience.

In conclusion, when it comes to field trips, using the above ideas will ensure that the experience is meaningful and positive for all involved. Remind your students to use their manners and thank the bus driver, tour guides, and anyone else who contributes to this special occasion. Upon returning, it is wise to create extension activities based upon the trip. This may include descriptive paragraphs or creating a travel brochure of the destination.

For most students, a field trip is one of the most memorable events of the school year. When planned properly, they will be enjoyable events for you, too!

Perhaps it was my catholic school upbringing that created my desire to have things in order. The day of my first official field trip was no different. Twenty-eight excited second graders and a dozen chaperones were eagerly awaiting the arrival of the buses.

As we waited, I noticed their quiet voices gradually getting louder and had a horrible vision; one hour, trapped in a hot, yellow school bus, with the shrill voices of little children. When I snapped out of it, I devised my School Trip Policy.

I told the students that, as we boarded the bus, I would show them to their seats. I also decided that the loading of the bus, the ride, and the unloading of the bus would be silent. My announcement certainly grabbed their attention and that of the parents. Of course, the students protested and a few parents raised their eyebrows. I told the students that they could read, sleep, look out the window, or think!

While it took several reminders, it was probably the best bus ride I had ever taken. The bus driver turned around several times to see if we were still there. As we arrived, the students were calm and well behaved. In addition, the bus driver commented that the silence helped her to do her job safely.

Word about the Silent Bus spread throughout the school quickly. The following year, my students were excited to be on the quiet bus and the only person who broke the rule was a parent who tried to start a round of 'Row, row, row your boat.' The poor man did not know about my policy until 3 students turned around and shushed him! - LW

Chapter 13

The Nuts And Bolts

Look Before You Leap

From the moment you accept your new teaching position, you need to be aware of the rights and responsibilities that you also accept. You are responsible for the education and safety of your students and must take this obligation seriously. While you deliberately try to follow every rule, you will notice some teachers who bend the rules. Do not model this behavior. If something were to happen, you cannot use the excuse that everyone else does it. You will be held accountable for not following procedure.

Whether you are teaching in a public school with a strong union or in a small, private school with no union, every teacher has rights. Belonging to a union provides a sense of security in areas previously unfamiliar to you. When issues arise, a union stands behind you, looking out for your best interest. You should, however, keep one thing in mind. A union protects your rights. A union cannot undo actions deemed inappropriate, incompetent, or dangerous to your students. The best thing you can do, to help your union help you, is to know and follow district policies to the letter. Read your contract and become familiar with the practices of your district. Attention to detail and a positive work ethic will be your best strategy for avoiding reprimands. Attend union meetings and know your rights. A common misconception is that non-tenured teachers do not have rights. This is untrue and it is worth your time to attend any workshops or presentations that focus on new teachers. If a situation arises and you are unsure of your rights, contact your union representative for immediate assistance.

While it is necessary to become familiar with your rights, it is as necessary to become familiar with your responsibilities. A competent new teacher strives to meet and exceed the expectations of students and administrators. There are many ways to combine effective teaching with successful classroom management skills. The following ideas will help you navigate day-to-day activities:

Arrive Early And Stay Late

There are many things that cannot be done when the children are present and staying later will allow you to straighten up your room, grade papers, and prepare for the next day. This is also a great time to get to know other staff members and learn from their experience.

Don't Wait For An Invitation

Turn in all documents, including lesson plans, attendance sheets, and report cards, on time. Do not wait until your name is called.

Bite Your Tongue

Avoid screaming and speaking to children in a derogatory manner. All children are sensitive, even those who will frustrate you the most. Always maintain your composure and remember that you are working with children.

Never Touch A Child

You probably remember your own teachers hugging you when you were upset or sick, and you probably never gave it a second thought.

Unfortunately, times have changed. Teachers now face the possibility that a reassuring hug could result in a lawsuit and the end of a career. It may seem harsh, but this is the reality of the world in which we live.

Be Aware Of Your Words

Be aware of the language you use in the presence of your students. Never use language that you would not use with your grandmother!

Speak Responsibly

Do not discuss adult topics or share intimate details of your life. This seems quite obvious when you are teaching first grade; however, high school students will want to know all about you and may ask very personal questions. Use discretion and common sense.

You Are Not A Taxi

Do not drive a student in your car. Once again, you may remember staying after school to help a teacher and having that teacher offer you a ride home. Today, this practice will open you, your school, and your district to a lawsuit. Never place a student in your car.

Do Not Let Your Guard Down

Never leave your students unattended, even for a moment. If you need to leave your room, be sure someone certified is there to supervise your class. Do not have a student supervise the class, you will be inviting trouble. *If anything happens while you are out of the room, you will be liable.*

Keep Your Eyes Peeled

Recess is for students, not for teachers. When your students are having recess, in a parking lot or a playground, you need to keep an eye on each student. Do not stand with other teachers assuming problems will not occur. Unstructured recess can pose many opportunities for conflict or injury. You must supervise your class at all times.

He Said, She Said

Until now, your school experience has been that of a student. Once you are hired for your first teaching position, your experience and perspective dramatically change.

School As A Workplace

To begin, your school will become your workplace. It is imperative that you conduct yourself as a professional at all times. This includes learning the chain of command and where specific questions should be directed. It is also important to ask questions. This is not a sign of weakness; it shows a desire to master your profession and an attention to detail. You will be given an enormous amount of information, and you should make a habit of writing down the answers to your questions and keeping them in a special folder for quick reference.

Politics, Gossip, and Drama

As a new teacher you will be immersed in much more than your classroom. You will be exposed to numerous coworkers, personalities and practices. From this perspective, working in a school will be quite similar to working in an office. You will encounter politics, gossip, and drama. You should do your best to avoid becoming involved in any of these situations.

First Impressions

Throughout the first year, your evaluations will not be limited to your principal. From the first day, you will be scrutinized by your peers, your students, and their parents. First impressions are important and you do not want to earn a negative label. The following are tips for successfully integrating yourself in your new workplace:

Put On Your Ears

New teachers should be seen and not heard. While this is an exaggeration, the general idea should be heeded. A new teacher who is fresh out of college and has no experience should never give unsolicited advice to veteran teachers. There is a huge difference between the theories you learn in college and the practical application of those theories. Veteran teachers know the students, the curriculum, and school policies. While you may not immediately understand why certain things occur as they do, there is probably a good, practical reason. Refrain from offering new ways to perform various tasks.

Patience Is A Virtue

Be patient. As you prepare your room in the summer, you will meet a number of teachers. Some will offer you assistance and encouragement, some may be indifferent, and some may be quite distant. Continue to be pleasant and approachable. If assistance is offered, accept it graciously and be open to suggestions. Understand that during the summer, teachers are often trying to get in and out of the building and enjoy the remainder of their summer break. In addition, many people need time to get to know someone. You are new in the building and will have to prove yourself. You may also be replacing a beloved colleague, and it will take time for people to accept a new person.

Many New Faces

During the summer, staff members drift in and out of the building and the environment is extremely casual. Some teachers will stop by your room to wish you well and introduce themselves. When someone enters your room, stop what you are doing and give him or her your full attention. Even though you will be meeting numerous people, do your best to remember their names. It helps to pay close attention when you are introduced and write their name and description down when they leave.

Reserve Judgement

Unfortunately, this is also the time when veteran teachers may begin to share information about colleagues with you. They may discuss the teacher next door to you and how he cannot control his class or the teacher down the hall who is always late. New teachers are often bombarded with gossip and your reaction should remain the same. **Listen, smile, and never comment under any circumstances**. It will take you most of the year to get an accurate read on your new colleagues. If you join in the gossip and discuss people you barely know, your comments may come back to haunt you. Regardless of public opinion, give each staff member a chance, and even if someone is blatantly rude to you, refrain from commenting about it to others.

Teach and Learn

Even though you are now a teacher, view your first year as a learning experience. You will not only learn to apply your teaching skills, you will learn to co-exist with numerous personalities. The most important thing to remember is that you will not love each person and each person will not love you. This is okay. There is a difference between establishing a close friendship and maintaining working relationships. While you will no doubt become close with some teachers, you should work at having a professional relationship with everyone in your building. This is accomplished by being pleasant, flexible, and refraining from gossip.

Stay Out Of The Headlines

Within a matter of weeks, you will learn of the labels teachers have been assigned. You may hear that Teacher B is wonderful and a hard worker or that Teacher C is moody and argumentative. The list goes on. Teachers are labeled for their personalities, their effectiveness, and their classroom management. Do your best to avoid a negative label. Arrive early, work hard, and assist others when you can. You do not want to be labeled a 'know-it-all' or a 'trouble-maker.' Strive to earn a positive reputation.

Do As I Say...

Politics is an area that few new teachers give much thought to, but exists in schools. Despite the rules, there is a pecking order, of sorts, and you will soon know who can get away with what. One teacher may never be reprimanded for leaving his class unattended. Another teacher may be reprimanded for bringing her class to lunch 3 minutes late. It may not seem fair and often times, it is not. Your best bet is to diligently follow all of the rules and refrain from publicly acknowledging that these relationships exist. Some call it playing dumb, but on the contrary, it is playing it smart.

Beware of Alliances

Just as it is wise to avoid gossip and politics, it is equally to your advantage to avoid joining a clique. Doing so in your first year may alienate you from many other staff members and until you get a chance to know everyone, it's hard to know who you will want to befriend. If you can work well with everyone, you will not need to belong to a clique.

Things Aren't Always As They Seem

Be sensitive to the fact that a colleague who appears indifferent to you may be going through a personal crisis, such as a divorce or an illness. As a new staff member, this is information the individual is not likely to divulge to you, so withhold judgment.

You Can Please Some Of The People...

Accept the fact that you cannot please everyone. You were hired to teach, that is job number one. Integrating yourself into the workplace is important, but no matter how hard you try, some people may not like you. Regardless of their treatment, continue to be professional and mature. Always take the high road.

If You Can't Say Something Nice...

Never, under any circumstances, discuss staff members in a negative way with students, parents, or administration. There is an unwritten rule that staff members keep disagreements *in house*. Go out of your way to mask any distaste for a coworker.

Mum Is The Word

Never discuss a student or parent in a negative way with your colleagues. You were probably warned in college that you do not discuss students in the teachers' room. This is excellent advice. Negative comments should be withheld from casual conversations. If you need to discuss an issue regarding a student or parent with a colleague, do so in private.

If Everyone Jumps Off A Bridge...

Do not model teachers who regularly break the rules. They may get away with it, as they are not being scrutinized as closely as you are. More than likely, you will not get away with it. Even if several teachers break a rule, do your best to follow the rules to the letter. This will eliminate problems in the future.

Time Will Tell

During your first year, you should spend most of your time listening, learning about others, and forming opinions based upon your own personal experiences. You may find that as you get to know everyone, you may form a close bond with someone you initially thought you would not like.

A Little Kindness Goes A Long Way

Courtesy is another way to show that you are a professional. If you use all of the paper in the copy machine, replace it before you leave. If you borrow an item from a teacher or the office, return it as soon as you are finished. This is a simple way to show other people respect.

Depending upon the size of your school, you may be part of a unit. Schools, with more than one class per grade level, generally establish grade level units. Your unit can be a tremendous source of advice and resources. Since the members of your unit are familiar with the curriculum and age level you are responsible for, they will be able to answer many of your questions. Be courteous and flexible. If you have a great worksheet, make copies for everyone in your unit and drop them in their mailboxes. Include a note that says you thought they might find the sheets useful. This is a great, non-threatening way to contribute to your unit and become a part of the team.

On Your Mark, Get Set, Teach!

Chapter 14

To Stay Or Not To Stay...
This Is The Question

While you will be evaluated, judged, and scrutinized throughout your first year of teaching, do not forget to turn the magnifying glass in the opposite direction. That is to say, make your own evaluations and judgments regarding your surroundings, too. When you are hired for your first teaching position, you will feel overwhelmed and anxious. As the year progresses, you should begin to feel more comfortable. If however, you are frequently uncomfortable or extremely stressed, you should begin to ask yourself some difficult questions.

The most important thing is to be honest with yourself regarding your performance, effort, and ability. The best way to conduct an accurate evaluation is to keep a journal throughout the school year. While this may sound like one more thing that you do not have time to complete, self-evaluation can have dramatic effects on your teaching career. The ability to evaluate yourself will allow you to self-correct and adapt. Here are some ideas for a **Self-evaluation Journal.**

There's No Place Like Home

Keep your journal at home. Do not bring it to school. It is a highly personal item that you would not want read by your colleagues or even worse, your students. This is especially important as you will not only evaluate your own behavior, but also the relationships you have with others. Naming names in a personal journal is acceptable, however irreversible damage could occur if those mentioned were aware that they were discussed in a negative manner.

Slam Books Are For Junior High

The primary focus of a self-journal is to evaluate *yourself*. In doing so, your interaction with others will be a large part of this process, but only as connected to you. This is not a junior high slam book or a clever way to remember spicy gossip. Your self-journal should be limited to your performance, relationships, and feelings. If done correctly, it will provide you with a valuable tool and ensure your growth as a professional.

Casual, Yet Practical

When you start your journal, be sure you date each entry. The timeline of occurrences is crucial and by the end of the year, the beginning of the year looks quite fuzzy. Since you will not be sharing your journal with anyone, you do not have to worry about grammar, spelling, or even writing in complete sentences. You are also under no obligation to write everyday. Such a schedule would be unrealistic and would surely lead to 'journal burnout' by October. It is much better to have a clear journal of important points that spans the course of the school year, than have every detail chronicled to November.

Bull's Eye

As mentioned above, there are three areas, performance, classroom management, and interaction, where you should target your efforts when evaluating your methods and effectiveness. You should focus on each area and make note of progress, changes, and difficulties.

Performance

The first area is performance. Performance is simply the instruction, classroom management, and emotional support you provide to your students. There are numerous ways to evaluate the success of your delivery and interactions.

Visual Assessment

You can visually assess the reaction of your students to your instruction, commands, or comments. Students that respect an instructor will not roll their eyes, sigh loudly, or slam books to show their distaste. *Your students will not always like you and this is normal.* The real question is, do they respond even when they are not happy? Do they heed directions? Do they seem to grasp the work you have assigned? Are they participating in a class discussion? Is it the same two students who always respond, or do they all contribute? Do they seem comfortable, uncomfortable, or too comfortable in class?

Classwork, Homework, Tests

Another way to evaluate your performance is by their classwork, homework, and tests. Tests should never be regarded as the sole criteria for assessment; however, combined with classwork and homework, tests will provide a more accurate, well-rounded picture. Be honest with yourself. Did a lesson go the way you imagined and planned it? Often times, as a result of many factors, this is not the case. Whether the students have not grasped the concept, do not enjoy the material, feel sick, feel tired, are bothered by the heat, or are looking forward to Halloween, lessons rarely go off *exactly* as planned. There are too many variables. The issue should not be whether the lesson plan was executed as specified in the lesson plan and teacher's manual. The issue is whether or not you have adjusted to the ever-changing needs of your class at any given time. If you are having trouble here, note where the lesson begins to deviate from the plan and why that makes *you* feel uncomfortable.

Classroom Management

The next item that should be examined is classroom management. You do not need a PhD in Child Psychology to determine if your classroom management skills are effective. If they are, you should continue to chronicle your practices and evaluate their success. If however, you know that your efforts are not working, you must go one step further. You need to examine *why* your management style is not effective and determine *how* to remedy the situation. Begin by asking yourself the following questions and use your observations to form accurate answers:

❖ Is the problem limited to a few difficult students or is the majority of the class out of control?

❖ Have you reviewed your rules?

❖ Do your students understand what you expect of them?

❖ Do they understand the consequences?

❖ Are the consequences appropriate for the offense?

❖ Have you followed through consistently?

❖ Are you firm?

❖ Have you discussed your difficulties with other staff members or administrators?

To properly improve your methods, you must be able to diagnose the problems. This is often a difficult task, as it requires you to find your own flaws in order to help your students. When faced with a difficult situation, all too often we look to assign blame. We feel a need to explain why something occurs as it does. Looking inward, to your own strengths and weaknesses, will produce something more important than blame. As a result, you will also gain perspective and find solutions. You may want to ask yourself the following questions:

❖ Am I too passive?

❖ Am I too aggressive?

❖ Am I consistent?

❖ Have I established a level of mutual respect with all of my students?

❖ Am I sensitive to their feelings and situations they may experience at home?

❖ Are my expectations realistic?

❖ Have I formatted my instruction to decrease distractions and elevate student interest?

❖ Are my lessons varied and interesting?

❖ Have I constructed my classroom in a manner conducive to learning?

❖ What could I do differently?

If you address each of these areas and there are a few students that continue to disrupt your lessons, you need to evaluate these particular students on an individual basis. Try the following:

❖ Begin by checking their permanent records. This will allow you to determine if the problems are new or pre-existing. By reading the comments of former teachers, you gain insight into a student's maturity and behavior patterns.

❖ You should also speak to former teachers, if possible. There may be significant circumstances that are contributing to the behavior.

❖ Another effective method of learning about students is to meet with the parent(s). Keep in mind that this is not always the most objective way to obtain pertinent information and that many parents are in denial or unsure of how to help their child.

❖ If the negative behavior persists, speak to the principal or school guidance counselor to determine if the student should be evaluated by the Child Study Team. Again, the records you keep will be crucial in assisting your students.

Interaction

The final area you will need to examine is the way you interact with students on an emotional level. Children, especially younger ones, are impacted by their teachers and you need to be aware of this. When you are under pressure or having a bad day, you cannot take this frustration out on your students. There is also a significant amount of down time during the day. This is the time when you are not formally instructing your class. Whether it is on the playground or between classes, you should attempt to establish a rapport with each student.

The best way to start a dialog with students is to ask them questions about things that interest them. You will find that your students will want to share the most minute details of their lives with you. Even if you are bored to tears, try to act enthusiastic and genuine. What may be painfully boring to you, is no doubt very important to the student. If your own child were in school, you would expect his or her teacher to be patient and interested. Treat each of your students as if they were your own children.

When you evaluate this area of your teaching experience, you will need to use a different set of criteria. There are no standardized tests to measure a teacher's emotional connection with his or her students. Instead, ask yourself these questions:

- ❖ Have I made a connection with each student?

- ❖ Have I gone out of my way to learn about their lives outside of school?

- ❖ Do I address problems they may be having and try to provide appropriate assistance?

- ❖ Have I favored any student in particular?

If you have favored a student, you could build resentment toward that student and yourself. If you know very little about certain students, you will need to work on establishing connections.

It must be noted that this is a much easier task for elementary school classroom teachers who spend the day with a small group of children. The good news is that even specialists or middle and high school subject teachers can establish these connections. In this case, much of the information will come from class discussions and meetings with students and will no doubt take much longer.

By maintaining a journal and following these tips, you will be able to monitor your progress as a new instructor and address any areas of weakness. The journal should also include your relationships with others and your feelings about your work environment.

When A Contract Is Offered

You will know, before the end of the year, if the school is going to offer you a contract for the upcoming year. Before this point, you should have a good idea as to whether or not this will occur, based upon observations by your administrator, staffing issues, and the upcoming budget. While you have been under the magnifying glass for a full year, you should be making your own evaluations. Do not sign on for another year if you have not given it serious thought. For many new teachers, there is no question as to whether they would like to continue in their position. For others, you may want to honestly evaluate your experience. You should not remain in a district, school, grade level, or subject that is not compatible with your personality, work ethic, and ability. It is hard to imagine sending out resumes and starting over in a new school, but if you were not happy with your environment, you should not stay.

Teachers who stay in unsatisfying positions incur much more stress, transfer their unhappiness to their students and staff members, and suffer from burnout. This is not an issue of right or wrong, but it is an issue of personal preference. Continuing to teach where you are not happy will have a negative impact on your students and influence their impression of school. It will also impact your life with your own family. The following are some questions you should ask yourself if you are not sure about continuing in your school:

Have I taught a grade level I am comfortable with?

Not everyone is comfortable teaching Kindergarten or 12th grade calculus. If you enjoy your school, but not your grade level, find out if there will be openings in different levels. If there are openings, inform your principal that you may be interested in changing grades. If not, stop by the Human Resources Department and find out if any other schools in your district will have openings in your level of interest.

Do I feel comfortable in my building?

Again, not everyone will feel comfortable in the same place. If you do not feel comfortable, try to assess the reasons. Have you tried to get to know others? Have you refrained from participating in gossip? Have you worked hard and assisted others when needed? The sad truth is that sometimes, regardless of your effort, it is nearly impossible to fit into a given area. If you feel that you have tried your best and have examined the relationships, then perhaps it is time to move on.

Have you received support from your administrator?

This is an area that should not be overlooked. Principals are people and they all have different personalities. When you click with a principal and feel that he or she is there to support and guide you, it is a wonderful feeling. Conversely, if an administrator is indifferent or argumentative, you may feel as though you have no security. As a new teacher, you want your administrators to notice the work you are doing and provide feedback. Whether that feedback is positive or negative, it is the manner in which it is delivered that will matter most.

In addition, you can ask yourself the following questions:

- ❖ Are you satisfied with the district in which you teach?
- ❖ Do you have the resources that you need?
- ❖ Does the district support the work that the teachers perform in the classroom?
- ❖ Is the district too large and do you prefer a small district where you work with the key players personally?

These are all personal preference questions that new teachers must answer for themselves. The following factors should be examined when considering the demands of an extensive commute:

Distance

Often, when prospective teachers begin sending out resumes, they tend to send many more than they originally anticipate. There is a high level of anxiety that they may not find a position and will face an uncertain future. To offset their anxiety, perspective teachers begin sending resumes to schools that are farther than they would like to travel. If you are hired by a school that is an hour away, you must take many things into consideration.

Weather

You will be driving everyday and regardless of weather, you will be expected to be on time.

Time

You will spend a great deal of time commuting, leaving less time to grade papers and prepare for the next day.

Evening Events

You will be expected to attend evening events, such as Back-To-School Night, Parent Teacher Conferences, Plays, etc. If you live far away, you will likely remain in the school or at a restaurant, rather than driving home and back again. A day that starts out with a 6:30 a.m. commute may not end until 10:30 p.m.

Future Plans

If you are single, it may be okay to work in a district that is far from home. If you marry and have children, this distance may become problematic. The commute is time away from your loved ones and can create an added measure of job-related stress.

The final question is simple. *Are you happy?* Be reasonable in your assessment of this question. No matter where you work, especially as a teacher, you will experience frustration, stress, and headaches. The important question is, are the rewards worth the frustration? The majority of teachers will assure you that this is the case. It is too difficult and important a career to just go through the motions. Teachers find satisfaction in seeing students achieve, improve, and grow. There are few careers where you can directly impact the lives of others as much as in education. When you assess your experience, examine the overall picture, not a bad day or week. As the year ends, are you already thinking about new ways to teach various topics or about new materials you cannot wait to purchase?

If you look forward to starting the next year, after an enjoyable summer of course, then you are probably in a good environment and have successfully completed Year 1! If you are dreading the thought of September and the first day of school, ask yourself the following questions:

Are you teaching the right level or subject for you?

Perhaps it is not teaching that you dislike, but the grade level or subject matter may be the problem. If you are a classroom teacher, maybe you would do better to specialize and teach one subject in a middle school or high school or become a specialist. This may involve returning to college, but it will be worth it if it makes you happy.

Would you prefer to work in a different capacity?

Perhaps you would be better suited as a Counselor, Speech Therapist, or Disciplinarian. Again, this may require that you return to school, but it could make all the difference and you will still be an integral part of the educational system.

Finally, the question you may be dreading -
Do you want to be a teacher?

It is not uncommon for someone to graduate from college and find a job in his or her field and be unhappy. This is the reason so many new teachers are not fresh college graduates, but mid-career transfers from every occupation under the sun. If you are really not happy, do yourself and your potential students a favor and find a job that will make you genuinely happy. There is no shame in finding out that what you were sure you wanted to be is not what you expected. The shame is in continuing.

Things Aren't Always What They Seem

The most important lesson of this chapter is that the decision to continue is two-sided. As a mature, college-educated individual, you have to ask yourself hard questions and answer them honestly. You should also consider that, for any number of reasons, a principal may not offer you a contract. It may be the result of budget cuts or the reason may be more complicated. Perhaps your principal has noticed your affinity for science and recommends that you teach in a middle school, where a significant emphasis is placed on science as opposed to the limited science curriculum in 1st grade. Just as you evaluate your strengths and weaknesses, your administrator will do the same. This type of advice is given with your best interest in mind and should be considered.

There are times when a new teacher is let go as a result of performance. This is not common, however, as weaknesses are usually addressed throughout the year. If you have graduated from college and worked very hard throughout your first year, you must be serious about teaching. If that is the case, you will no doubt work to improve yourself and earn a position for the following year.

The Tenure Myth

Many people think of tenure as the magical time where you must be hired and cannot be easily dismissed. It would behoove any teacher that is part of a union or teaches in a tenured district to learn about tenure.

There is a common misunderstanding of the concept. People often think that new teachers are extremely vulnerable and tenured teachers have the run of the house. The truth is, non-tenured teachers do have rights and conversely, tenured teachers must continue to excel and perform, follow the rules, and adhere to district policy. A principal with a well-documented case can and will dismiss a tenured teacher that does not fulfill his or her obligations.

In conclusion, education is the cornerstone of any society and should be regarded as the preparation for our future. Work hard, ask questions, and let common sense guide you throughout your career. Your first year as a new teacher will be your most memorable. Try to enjoy your students and the career you have chosen. Remember, this is not a sprint...it's a marathon!

On Your Mark, Get Set, Teach!

Chapter 15

May We Suggest?

As a new teacher, you may not be aware of the wonderful resources the world of education has to offer. Happily, as a result of the technological boom, resources are abundant, inexpensive (sometimes free), and require little effort to obtain.

Do Not Make This At Home

The days of homemade alphabets and stencils are long gone. When you are looking for creative decorations or addition problems for second graders, our advice remains constant - do not make this at home. There was a time when teachers lovingly handcrafted the letters displayed on bulletin boards. These same teachers would use blank ditto master sheets to prepare a math quiz or language test. Fortunately, times have changed! Welcome to the world of pop-out letters, black-line reproducibles, and the Internet.

❖   A simple Internet search will provide you with more information than you will ever need for a given topic. Whether your students are studying apples or anatomy, you will find information, lesson plans, and ideas to deliver extraordinary lessons. Thirty years ago students had access to outdated encyclopedias with a few paragraphs about a topic. Now students can locate thirty-thousand references for that same topic!

❖   A virtual visit to any educational supplier will have your order on your doorstep within a day or two. You can easily order charts, posters, stationary, reproducible books, supplemental materials, and decorations, often at a discount.

❖   And finally, a trip to your local teacher's store will yield even more. In addition to the supplies and equipment, you will have access to teachers. The majority of staff members in educational stores were or still are teachers. They become a terrific resource and well worth the trip. Unlike giant superstores, service is a key element and you will feel it the moment you walk in the door. If you need materials for a unit on rocks, they will be able to point out more than where they are located; they can tell you which items work best.

What's In Store?

Before long, you will see the lengths most educators will go to in order to help a fellow teacher. If you are starting to wonder how you will be able to repay everyone who helps you, the answer is simple. As you gain experience, be sure that you help other new teachers. It is that simple. Do not forget how you felt your first year. Once you have been teaching for a while, there may be times when you begin to lose your patience with a new teacher. This is when you need to remember how apprehensive that person must feel.

The Moment We've All Been Waiting For...

In an effort to provide you with a comprehensive list of resources, we have devoted an entire chapter to this endeavor.

We begin with a list of Internet resources that provide lesson plans, content information, and links to a multitude of valuable sites. Many will have postings allowing new teachers from across the country and the world to communicate, ask questions, and solve problems together.

The second section is a list of websites that offer Teacher Freebies. Yes, you read it correctly. You should, however, remember your grandmother's advice about free lunches. Even though the materials are free, there is usually a good reason that they are giving them away. Many times they are an advertisement or part of a promotion. If a company or association is giving away free materials, they may be trying to shape young minds. Examine materials carefully and if there is another side to the story, present that to your students also.

Finally, the Teacher's Store Directory, is listed by state, with information about each store. While it may be tempting, at times, to save money and create decorations or reproducible materials by hand, you may want to weigh the time involved with the money you are saving. You will surely find that the materials you are creating can be purchased inexpensively, leaving you more time to prepare your lessons or dare we say it, relax!

Use this book as a tool to develop meaningful instruction, effective classroom management, and positive relationships with your students, their parents, and your school community. This chapter provides the resources that will enable you to make your first year of teaching a success. In conclusion, take a deep breath, exhale, and know that you will do great!

Internet Resources

The Internet is one of the most valuable tools available for *all* teachers, but especially *new teachers*. As you browse through these sites, you will find links to additional sites. While we could not include all of the 1,000,000+ websites that we came across, we have compiled a list that we are sure you will find valuable.

❖ Franklin Mason Press Guest Young Author & Illustrator Contest
 www.franklinmasonpress.com

❖ Web Resources for Teachers and Students
 www.i-55.com/lynnfleming/bm.htm

❖ Really Good Stuff
 http://www.reallygoodstuff.com

❖ A#1 Teacher Resource For Teachers
 www.infolinee.officehiway.com/teacher_resources.htm

❖ RHL School
 www.rhlschool.com/

❖ Sites For Teachers
 www.sitesforteachers.com

❖ The Discovery Channel Website
 http://school.discovery.com/teachers

❖ Teaching Treasures
 www.teachingtreasures.com.au/

❖ Education World
 http://www.educationworld.com

❖ International Reading Association
 www.reading.org/links/edu_tp.html

❖ Teacher Zone
   http://www.teacherzone.com

❖ A-OK Teacher Stuff
   www.aokteacherstuff.com/language_resources.htm

❖ School Express
   http://www.schoolexpress.com/

❖ Teacher Resources That Save Time
   http:www.timesaversforteachers.com/

❖ SIRS Web Resources for Teachers
   www.sirs.com/wrc/teachers.htm

❖ The World of Math Online
   www.math.com/teachers/centers.html

❖ Math Goodies
   www.mathgoodies.com/teachers.htm

❖ A to Z Teacher Stuff
   http://www.atozteacherstuff.com/

❖ FEMA For Kids
   www.fema.gov/kids/teachers.htm

❖ National Geographic
   www.nationalgeographic.com/education/

❖ PBS Television Links
   www.pbs.org/teachersource/

❖ Nickelodeon
   http://teachers.nick.com/

❖ K-8 Education Place
   www.eduplace.com/

❖ Character Education
   www.goodcharacter.com/

❖ The Write Source
   http://www.the write source.com

❖ Articles for Teachers
   www.virtu-software.com/articles

❖ Teachers at Random
   www.randomhouse.com/teachers

❖ Scholastic
   http://teacher.scholastic.com

❖ Teacher Resources
   www.mikids.com/teacher.html

❖ Teacher Information Network
   http://www.teacher.com/

Free Resources

❖ What is Free? Federal Resources For Educational Excellence
    www.ed.gov/free/new.htm/

❖ ABC Teach
    www.abcteach.com

❖ Free Resources for Teachers
    www.garvick.com/freebies/teachers.htm

❖ Free Lesson Plans
    www.edhelper.com/

❖ NEA Free Education Resources
    www.nea.org/grants/free.html

❖ Links To Free Resources For Teachers
    www.emunix.emich.edu/vhughes/free/

❖ Free Teacher Resource Index
    http://freebies.about.com/cs/teachersfreebies

❖ Free Things For Educators
    www.freethings4educators.com/

❖ Free Teaching Aids
    www.freeteachingaids.com

❖ Free Resources for Parents and Educators
    www.parenting-resources.com/free_resources.htm

Directory of Teacher's Stores

On Your Mark, Get Set, Teach!

The following directory is of significant importance to all teachers, especially those at the beginning of their careers. Teacher's stores are much more than the products they carry. They offer ideas, advice from educators on staff, and creative products to save you time and energy.

As you begin your career, you will soon understand why most teachers do not have summer villas in Spain. While some supplies are provided by the school district, many of the materials you will use to supplement instruction and create a pleasant environment are not. For a new teacher, it may seem expensive at times, however, the expense must be weighed against your time. You may think you are saving money by making homemade materials or decorations, but think twice. Your time is extremely valuable and you should not spend hours on a project that could be purchased inexpensively.

There is good news. If you take care of the materials you purchase, you will soon amass quite a collection, requiring less expense each year. Laminate posters, keep alphabets and borders in airtight containers, and avoid tearing pages out of reproducible books.

The following is a comprehensive directory of teacher's stores from practically every state. While there are many wonderful stores, catalogs, and websites not listed, we felt that the stores listed include the best of the educational supply market. If you live in one of the few states not listed, do not fret. Many of the stores offer catalogs, online viewing, and online purchasing, allowing you to have your order delivered to your doorstep. In addition, many offer discounts or gifts to teachers. If possible, we do suggest that you visit these wonderful stores. Their knowledge and expertise will be invaluable and you will be inspired when you see all they have to offer.

The stores are listed by state and all information was up-to-date at the time of printing. It is wise, however, to call before visiting a store, to confirm the location and the hours.

ALABAMA

Off Campus, Inc.
www.edumart.com/offcampus

Whoa! Browse no further. We are your one stop teacher shop with over 25 years experience in teacher and educational supplies. We offer a **10% discount** on all online buys and **FREE** delivery for local customers. We guarantee quality product selection, low prices, and 100% satisfaction.

480 George Wallace Dr.
Gadsen, AL 35903
Tel. 256-547-0505
Fax 256-547-0579

ALASKA

Schoolhouse Express
www.schoolhouseexpress.com
3 Locations

We are a full-line retailer of teacher aids, curriculum guides, classroom furniture and decorations, homeschool supplies, and more! Visit any of our three stores or shop our online catalog! Just click to shop.

Fairbanks Store
3415 Airport Way
Fairbanks, AK 99709
Tel. 907-456-8262
Toll Free (in Alaska only) 800-478-8262

Anchorage Store
2217 E. Tudor Rd. Ste. 9
Anchorage, AK 99507
Tel. 907-562-5557
Toll Free (in Alaska only) 800-540-5557

Wasilla Store
290 Yenlo St.
Wasilla, AK 99654
Tel. 907-357-6474
www.schoolhouseexpress.com

ARIZONA

Learning Is Fun
www.learningisfun.com
7 Locations in 5 States

Learning Is Fun provides teachers and parents with educational materials for the classroom and home. Our stores offer a wide product selection in a fun, well-organized place to shop. You'll find a cheerful staff, featured themes and special displays year-round, hundreds of new products each month, and everyday value pricing on supplies and other basics.

Village Fair Shopping Center
12643 N. 48th Street
Phoenix, AZ 85032
Tel. 602-996-4660
Fax 602-996-9307

Monkey Play Teaching Supplies
http://www.edumart.com/monkeyplay

Where learning is fun! Hop into Monkey Play. Stroll and dance around the aisles, pick up a whistle and maybe a smile. We have stickers, flashcards, name tags and borders. Jump up to the counter and let us take your orders. Happy Shopping!

1444 South 4th Avenue
Yuma, AZ 85364
Tel. 520-343-1999
Fax 520-343-1191

ARKANSAS

A+ Educational Supply
www.apluseducational.com

Owned and operated by a former teacher, our motto is, if it doesn't make learning fun, we don't have it! Known as one of the outstanding educational stores in the area, A+ offers a large selection of educational products, toys, games, office supplies, inspirational materials, and home-school materials. Shop our store or visit our *Online Catalogue!*

1401 North Main
Harrison, AR 72601
(Younces Shopping Center)
Tel. 870-741-1880
Fax 870- 741-2177

CALIFORNIA

CM School Supply
www.cmschoolsupply.com
4 locations to serve you:

Look no further! We have the largest selection of school supplies in Southern California. We strive to carry the materials you are looking for. Visit any of our four locations or take advantage of our online ordering with access to 1,000's of items with the click of your mouse.

Anaheim Store
1025 E. Orangethorpe Ave.
Anaheim, CA 92801
Tel. 714-680-6681
Fax 714-680-0963

NEW - Long Beach Store
5440 E. Del Amo Blvd.
Long Beach, CA 90808
Tel. 562-429-2425

Riverside
4301 Tyler St.
Riverside, CA 92503
Tel. 909-689-6400
Fax 909-689-6498

Upland
940 N. Central Ave.
Upland, CA 91786
Tel. 909-982-9695
Fax 909-982-6906

COLORADO

CONNECTICUT

Teacher Parent Store
www.zteacher.com/teacherparent-ct

In business over 22 years, our staff is comprised of educators ready to assist you in your educational shopping. Call for our 400 page catalog, drop by our store, or visit us on the web!

93 Mill Plain Road
Danbury, CT 06811
Tel. 203-794-0577
Fax 203-798-9854

DELAWARE

Classroom Corner

The largest selection of teaching materials in Sussex County, featuring products from over fifty companies. Special orders welcome and Home Schooling Curriculum available. Friendly staff and personal service are our specialty. Stop by and sign up for our Teacher Appreciation Club!

208 Main Street
Millsboro, DE 19966
Tel. 302-934-8119
Fax 302-934-8122

FLORIDA

Get Smart
www.getsmartsuperstores.com
4 locations to serve you:

Our 4 brick and mortar superstores, with a staff of over 70, are open 7 days (and nights) a week to serve you. Since 1979 we have been supplying the United States, Central and South America, and the Caribbean. Our export division is fluent in Spanish and we have educational resources for every market, including teachers, schools, and parents.

Dade - W. Kendall
8700 SWY 137th Court
Miami, FL 33183
Tel. 305-387-0834
Fax 305-383-8449

Dade - Pinecrest
11751 S. Dixie Highway
Miami, FL 33156
Tel. 305-378-0834
Fax 305-378-0124

Broward
8507 Pines Blvd.
Pembroke Pines, FL 33024
Tel. 954-431-5052
Fax 954-431-5089

Palm Beach
4366 Northlake Blvd.
Palm Beach Gardens, FL 33410
Tel. 561-691-0091
Fax 561-691-0076

GEORGIA

J&M's Teachers' Corner
Parent/Teacher Store
www.zteacher.com/jm-nc

218 S. Main Street
Hiawassee, GA 30546
Tel. 706-896-0064
Fax 706-896-0064
Toll Free 888-837-6599

We try hard to please each of our customers by covering all levels and areas of education. Our customers include homeschoolers, teachers, churches, and parents. Stop by our store, in Georgia or North Carolina, to speak with our knowledgeable staff or conveniently shop online.

Learning Tree Educational Resources, Inc.
www.mylearningtree.com

Supplying educators since 1979. Offering a full-line of instructional materials, teaching aides, and school supplies from a variety of traditional and innovative publishers and manufacturers.

281 Norman Drive
Valdosta, GA 31601
Tel. 229-244-9967
Toll Free 800-234-9967
Fax 229-245-7744

HAWAII

Education Works
www.educationworkshawaii.com

Hawaii's largest and most complete source of learning materials for teachers and parents. Shop with us for all of your educational needs, including classroom supplies, teaching materials, educational toys, games and so much more! Visit our store or shop on-line!

2850 Pukoloa Street
Suite 103
Honolulu, HI 96819
Tel. 808-564-2775
Fax 808-564-2825

IDAHO

Teaching World Resource Center
www.edumart.com/idteachingworld

222 3rd Ave S
Nampa, ID 83651
Toll Free 800-714-1403
Fax 208-465-1900

Teaching World Resource Center is the most progressive retail school supply store in Idaho. We offer a full-line of classroom enhancement for the public/private/homeschool classroom as well as creative curriculum resources. We have a variety of children's toys, literature, and hands-on learning materials for ages 1 to 101. We also offer private tutoring and informative workshops.

ILLINOIS

The Chalkboard
www.edumart.com/chalkboard
3 locations to serve you:

The Chalkboard offers an exciting product mix and the most complete collection of effective teaching tools, educational materials, and classroom supplies for children of all ages. Visit one of our 3 locations and take advantage of our in-store Chalkboard Cash program.

Joliet (Crest Hill)
2110 Plainfield Road
(Rt. 30)
Joliet, IL 60435
Tel. 815-741-2023

Naperville
1163 E. Ogden Ave
Iroquois Center #339
Naperville, IL 60563
Tel. 630-357-1690

Aurora
367 Rt. 59
Aurora Marketplace
Aurora, IL 60504
Tel. 630-585-8700

Let's Learn
www.letslearn.com
4 locations to serve you:

Let's Learn is a full-service retail store chain featuring thousands of educational products and materials for the classroom and home. We offer the largest selection of educational supplies in the Midwest from great manufacturers and we specialize in hard to find items.

Darien
Chestnut Court Shopping Center
7511 Lemont Rd.
Darien, IL 60561
Tel. 630-910-9999
Fax 630-910-7325

Hoffman Estates
The Golf Center
14 Golf Rd.
Hoffman Estates, IL 60195
Tel. 847-755-1115
Fax 847-755-1114

Rockford
Forest Plaza
6253 E. State St.
Rockford, IL 61108
Phone 815-226-8899
Fax 815-226-8460

West Dundee
Spring Hill Fashion Center
848 W. Main St.
West Dundee, IL 60118
Tel. 847-836-6200
Fax 847-836-9516

IOWA

University Book & Supply
www.panthersupply.com

University Book & Supply's mission is to be the superior provider of educational materials and related merchandise, exceeding our customers' expectations for quality, service, and value. We carry a wide selection of materials from many vendors for teachers and student teachers and have one of the largest children's book departments in the area.

1009 West 23rd Street
P.O. Box 486
Cedar Falls Iowa 50613
Tel. 319-266-7581
Toll Free 800-728-7581
Fax 319-277-1266

KENTUCKY

The Education Station

We strive to meet all of your educational needs, offering a 15% discount on school purchase orders. A variety of Christian materials available.

1584 Diederich Blvd
Russell, KY 41169
Tel. 606-883-8445
Fax 606-833-8455

MAINE

Play and Learn
Toys and Teaching Resources
www.playandlearn.me.homestead.com

Open seven days a week and conveniently located just off Exit 20 of I-95 in Freeport, Maine, Play and Learn is the largest independently-owned parent/teacher store in New England, with over 8,000 square feet of retail space on two floors devoted to the best products in specialty toys and educational materials.

140 Main Street
Freeport, ME 04032
Tel. 207-865-6434
Toll Free 888-865-6434
Fax 207-865-7010

MARYLAND

ABC's and 123's, Inc
http://hometown.aol.com/abc123inc/index.html

Teacher-owned and operated, serving the greater Washington DC area. Customer service oriented, we carry a wide variety of products to support the Montgomery County Schools. Sign up for our e-mail updates!

12219 Nebel St
Rockville, MD 20582
Tel. 301-881-5133
Fax 301-881-3764

On Your Mark, Get Set, Teach!

MASSACHUSETTS

Teachers Pet, Inc
www.zteacher.com/teacherspet-ma

The largest teacher supply store in New England with a staff of educators on hand to assist with questions or purchasing decisions. Shop our store or our extensive website!

360 Merrimack St
Lawrence, MA 01843
Tel. 978-681-0745
Fax 978-687-8622

MICHIGAN

Let's Learn
www.letslearn.com
3 locations to serve you:

Let's Learn is a full-service retail store chain featuring thousands of educational products and materials for the classroom and home. We offer the largest selection of educational supplies in the Midwest from great manufacturers and we specialize in hard to find items.

Grand Rapids
Plainfield Plaza
3170 Plainfield NE
Grand Rapids, MI 49525
Tel. 616-364-7660
Fax 616-361-5455

Grandville
Rivertown Center
3825 Rivertown Parkway, Suite 200
Grandville, MI 49418
Tel. 616-257-9595
Fax 616-257-6575

Holland
North Park Plaza
2337 North Park Drive
Holland, MI 49424
Tel. 616-355-2222
Fax 616-355-0048

The School House
www.edumart.com/schoolhousedet

We are a full service teacher, parent, and student store specializing in educational supplies, books and teaching aids to enhance the educational experience. We also offer educational games, posters, paper goods, art supplies, and furniture. Our main store in Detroit is an educational supermarket.

Livernois Avenue of Fashion
19363 Livernois
Detroit, MI 48221
Tel. 313-342-1261
Toll Free 800-342-1261
Fax 313-342-0188

Summit Place Mall
3-15-141 N. Telegraph Rd.
Waterford, MI 48328
Tel. 248-706-3452
Toll Free 800-342-1261
Fax 248-706-3458

MINNESOTA

Cool Cat School Supplies & Toys, In.c
www.edumart.com/classroomonwheels

Reasonable prices and FREE SHIPPING on all of our resource books, bulletin board and room decorations, stickers, craft supplies, manipulatives, games, and toys.

Fairbo West Mall - 200 Western Ave
Faribault, MN 55201
Tel. 507-332-Cool (2665)
Fax 507-335-5788

MISSISSIPPI

Fun Learning Stuff at Education Station
www.funlearningstuff.com

Our store is stocked with over 8,000 items, from charts, stickers, workbooks, children's literature, computer software, educational technology, pre-school supplies, furniture, equipment, art supplies, toys, games, and puzzles to home school products and homework helpers. Shop our store or our online catalogue.

1101 Belmont St
Vicksburg, MS 39180
Tel. 601-636-2926
Fax 601-636-2926

MISSOURI

Ann's Teacher Store
www.edumart.com/annsteachersstore

A full-line Teacher's Store. Come shop our online catalog with over 8,000 products or stop in our store and choose from a wide variety of educational products. If you cannot locate a product on our site, call our toll free line and we will be more than happy to help!

1004 W. Worley St
Columbia, MO 65203
Tel. 573-443-2667
Toll Free 800-431-1417
Fax 573-442-9699

NEBRASKA

The Creative Teacher
www.edumart.com/creativeteacher

The store with a wide range of educational resources, supplies, and gifts for teachers, parents, and students. Enjoy the convenience of online shopping or visit our store for friendly, personal, and helpful customer service.

2027 Central Avenue
Kearney, NE 68847
Tel. 308-236-5558
Toll Free 800-537-9060
Fax 308-236-0788

NEVADA

Learning Is Fun
www.learningisfun.com
3 locations to serve you:

Learning Is Fun provides teachers and parents with educational materials for the classroom and home. Our stores offer a wide product selection in a fun, well-organized place to shop. You'll find a cheerful staff, featured themes and special displays year-round, hundreds of new products each month, and everyday value pricing on supplies and other basics.

Henderson - Whitney Ranch Center
673 Stephanie St
Henderson, NV
Tel. 702-456-5437
Toll Free 800-290-5437
Fax 702-456-1294

Las Vegas - Decatur Crossing Center
290 S. Decatur Blvd
Las Vegas, NV 89107
Tel. 702-258-5437
Toll Free 800-290-5437
Fax 702-258-9695

Las Vegas - Boca Park Marketplace
8800 W. Charleston Blvd
Las Vegas, NV 89107
Tel. 702-873-5437
Toll Free 800-290-5437
Fax 702-952-0170

NEW HAMPSHIRE

Imagination Village
www.edumart.com/imaginationvillage

Imagination Village is owned and operated by a group of teachers and parents who are dedicated to providing outstanding educational materials that make learning exciting, motivating, and just plain fun! Our wide variety of products serve a diverse population of children, the academically gifted and those with special needs.

9 North Main St
Concord, NH 03301
Tel. 603-225-1060
Fax 603-225-0613

Keys To Learning
www.edumart.com/keys2learning

Keys To Learning is dedicated to providing teachers and parents with the latest, as well as tried and true educational games, toys, books and equipment to keep young minds challenged! Visit our website to checkout our workshop schedule, latest newsletter, full line catalog, sales, and specials. Help a child unlock the door to education with the Keys To Learning.

228 Daniel Webster Highway
Nashua, NH 03060
Tel. 603-888-3505
Fax 603-888-7121
Toll Free Tel. 888-teach-86
Toll Free Fax 888-200-8559

NEW JERSEY

Bordens
www.bordenstat.com

We are a family-owned business serving the New Jersey Shore since 1918. Now, due to modern technology, we are able to serve you with the same dedication, friendliness, and quality merchandise. If you are in the neighborhood, stop by and see us, or shop our full online catalogs.

601 Arnold Avenue
Point Pleasant, NJ 08742
Tel. 732-899-1234
Fax 732-899-4991

Learning Partners

We are central Jersey's one-stop shop for all your educational needs, with a staff of experienced teachers to help you. We carry materials for Pre-K through High School, including an extensive foreign language section. A store catalog is available for school purchase orders.

250 Rte 130
Bordentown, NJ 08505
Tel. 609-298-9224
Fax 609-298-9226

NEW MEXICO

Learning Is Fun
www.learningisfun.com

Learning is Fun provides teachers and parents with educational materials for the classroom and home. Our stores offer a wide product selection in a fun, well-organized place to shop. You'll find a cheerful staff, featured themes and special displays year-round, hundreds of new products each month, and everyday value pricing on supplies and other basics.

5000 Menaul Blvd NE
Albuquerque, NM 87110
Tel. 505-889-8860
Toll Free 888-913-5437
Fax 505-889-8875

NEW YORK

Teach N' Toys
www.teachntoys.com
2 locations to serve you:

Owner, Ricki Block, is a certified Speech Pathologist who can assist you in choosing appropriate materials for children with special needs. Visit our stores or shop our online catalog with thousands of educational products.

Orange County
318 Blooming Grove Tpk. (Rt. 94)
New Windsor, NY 12553
Tel. 914-565-2235
Toll Free 800-224 READ

Westchester County
2050 East Main Street
Cortlandt Manor, NY 10567
Tel. 914-788-5348
Toll Free 877-225 READ

The Parent Teacher Store

Two locations – each about 5,000 square feet, carrying a wide range of educational supplies and toys. Shop our stores, catalog, or secure website.

63 North Front Street
Kingston, NY 12401
Tel. 845-339-1442
Toll Free 800-598-5417
Fax 845-339-1467

515 Troy-Schenectady Road
Latham, NY 12110
Tel. 518-785-6272
Fax 518-785-0105

NORTH CAROLINA

J&M's Teacher's Corner
www.zteacher.com/jm-nc

For high levels of customer service, visit our GA or NC stores or conveniently shop online.
11 Highway 19 S.
Bryson City, NC 28713
Tel. 828-488-9161

NORTH DAKOTA

Art & Learn
www.edposters.com
2 locations to serve you:

Art & Learn specializes in educational supplies to meet the needs of today's teachers. Our experienced staff can assist our customers with knowledgeable suggestions and answers to your questions. Our Grand Forks store also carries an extensive selection of art supplies. We invite you to stop by our stores or visit our website.

Grand Forks
120 N. Washington Street
Grand Forks, ND 58203
Tel. 701-772-0927
Fax 701-772-1733

Fargo
1225 University Drive South
Fargo, ND 58103
Tel. 701-476-1988

OHIO

The Spelling Bee
www.edumart.com/spellingbee

Located in NW Ohio, The Spelling Bee is more than just a teacher's store. Visit us or shop online.

146 E. Main Street
Van Wert, Ohio 45891
Tel. 419-238-1018
Fax 419-238 1018

OKLAHOMA

The Apple Tree
www.edumart.com/theappletree

Learning materials for home, school, and church - meeting educational needs for all ages. Shop in our 10,000 square foot store, through our catalog, or online. Our friendly, knowledgeable staff will be happy to assist you with your educational needs.

7204 E. 41st Street
Tulsa, OK 74145
Tel. 918-622-8733
Fax 918-622-2482

PENNSYLVANIA

The Learning Source
http://www.edu-care.net/learningsource
2 locations to serve you:

Learning and fun for all ages and stages. Teachers, caregivers, parents, grandparents, and homeschoolers, shop us online or in our stores; we are your helpful source for everything educational.

Camp Hill
3401 Hartzdale Drive
Camp Hill, PA 17011
Tel. 717-761-7445

Harrisburg
5811 Old Jonestown Road
Harrisburg, PA 17112
Tel. 717-652-9467

RHODE ISLAND

Teachers Room Ltd.

Staff of educators ready to assist our customers, offering monthly promotions, special orders, and expert advice.

1395 Atwood Avenue
Johnston, RI 02919
Tel. 401-943-1424

SOUTH CAROLINA

Teacher's Touch, Inc.
www.teacherstouch.com

Extensive inventory of educational products and supplies for parents and teachers to purchase online or in our store with the help of our knowledgeable staff. We are the premier retail teaching supply store of Myrtle Beach, Horry County, and South Carolina.

2610 South King's Highway
Myrtle Beach, SC 29577
Tel. 843-448-4690
Fax 843-448-7029

SOUTH DAKOTA

Teaching Treasures

Experienced staff of educators available to assist with purchases and answer questions. Friendly, customer-oriented store serving the needs of teachers statewide. Open seven days a week.

1113 W. 41st Street
Sioux Falls, SD 57105
Tel. 605-332-8755

TENNESSEE

Bright Ideas
www.edumart.com/brightideas

Receive a 15% discount on all online orders. We offer all the educational and art materials that every teacher, parent, preschool, Sunday school, and homeschooler could need. Over 80,000 items available. If you do not see it, call our toll free number or e-mail your request. We are here to serve you.

3551 West Emory Road
Powell, TN 37849
Tel. 865-947-3030
Toll Free 800-729-7898 (US only)
Fax 865-947-3007

Learning House
www.edumart.com/learninghouseonline
3 locations to serve you:

Learning House provides the ultimate in learning products (Pre K - 12) for parents, schools, and churches. We have been a leader in the educational field for 18 years. One owner, one goal...to give our customers the best in service, selection and value.

Memphis
6135 Mt. Moriah Ext.
Memphis, TN 38115
Tel. 901-795-2610
Fax 901-795-2626

Barlett
2849 Barlett Blvd.
Barlett, TN 38115
Tel. 901-385-1519
Fax 901-385-1697

Germantown
3120 Village Shops Drive
Germantown, TN 38139
Tel. 901-737-6225
Fax 901-737-8769

Toll Free Outside Memphis 1-800-492-1899

TEXAS

A Teacher's Aide
www.ateachersaide.com

A Teacher's Aide offers teacher, parent, and educational supplies from over 200 manufacturers and publishers. We offer materials for pre-school through high school. We are an approved vendor for the Dallas Public Schools and most suburban districts.

6444B E. Mockingbird
Dallas, TX 75214
Tel. 214-826-8366

UTAH

Utah-Idaho School Supply
www.uisupply.com
Toll Free 1-800-348-8345
5 locations to serve you:

We have an experienced staff to assist you with your purchases, whether you choose to shop in one of our 5 stores or online. We are Utah's education location for teachers, parents, kids, and map enthusiasts.

Salt Lake City
2120 S 700 E Unit F
Salt Lake City, UT 84106
Tel. 801-474-2244

Layton
448 W Antelope Dr.
Layton, UT 84041
Tel. 801-779-2240

Murray
6562 So. State
Murray, Utah 84107
Tel. 801-262-0222

Ogden
2665 Washington Blvd.
Ogdon, Utah 84401
Tel. 801-621-5020

New Utah Valley
265 North State Street
Lindon, Utah 84042
Tel. 801-221-9963

VERMONT

A Teacher's Closet

67 Center Street
Rutland, VT 05701
Tel. 802-773-1377

VIRGINIA

Teachers Edition

1723 Concord Drive
Charlottesville, VA 22901
Tel. 434-296-3439
Fax 434-296-0499

WASHINGTON

Academic Toolbox
www.academictoolbox.com

The tools to combine learning and fun! Our full service retail store, serving North Central Washington, supplies educational materials for teachers, parents, preschools, Sunday schools, and homeschoolers, from infant to grade 12. Our website gives the same unmatched service to our friends throughout the country.

2127 N. Wenatchee Ave.
Wenatchee, WA 98801
Tel. 509-667-8746
Fax 509-663-0153

Learning Is Fun
www.learningisfun.com

Learning Is Fun provides teachers and parents with educational materials for the classroom and home. Our stores offer a wide product selection in a fun, well-organized place to shop. You'll find a cheerful staff, featured themes and special displays year-round, hundreds of new products each month, and everyday value pricing on supplies and other basics.

5414 E. Sprague Avenue
Spokane, WA 99212
Tel. 509-536-4900
Fax 509-536-0800

WEST VIRGINIA
The Teacher's Aid

Educational supplies for parents and teachers provided by a staff with teaching experience.

146 Park Shopping Center
Parkersburg, WV 26104
Tel. 304-422-0829
Fax 304-422-0820

WISCONSIN

Beacon Ridge
www.beacon-ridge.com

Unique classroom materials selected by an occupational therapists and team of educational consultants. Supplies to support handwriting and assistive technology solutions.

20951 Baker Road
Gays Mills, WI 54631
Tel. 608-734-9318
Fax 608-734-3720

A+ School Supplies
www.edumart.com/aplus

A+ Inc. simply the best place to get teacher and parent learning supplies! 10% OFF your entire online order. We will also ship all orders over $50.00 for FREE. In addition, each order over $50.00 receives a free gift!

Hales Corner
5720 S. 108th St.
Hales Corner, WI 53130
Tel. 414-427-8844
Fax 414-427-8899

WYOMING

Bailey School Supply, Inc.
www.baileysofficecity.com
520 S. Walnut
Casper, WY 82601
Tel. 307-265-4742
Toll Free 800-675-7509
Fax 307-234-0839

Working together to inspire the love of learning in young minds.